Praise For *I Even Regret Night:*
Holi Songs Of Demerara

"Through his songs, author Lalb...
to, validates, and pays tribute to a people's spiritual alchemy.
I Even Regret Night is the triumph of the pen over the whip.
It is the triumph of the dignity and self-respect of a people
over the conditions of degradation. It is the triumph of the
awakened inner spirit over the unconsciousness that threat-
ens to undermine and silence the oversoul of humanity."
—Deborah G. Plant, editor of *Barracoon: The Story of the
Last Black Cargo* by Zora Neale Hurston

"Rajiv Mohabir is the best kind of translator: he is well aware
of the ghosts—historical, linguistic, and personal—that
haunt the distance between these poems' mouths and our
humble ears."
—Kazim Ali, author of *SkyWard*

"In his Nobel acceptance speech, Derek Walcott spoke of
witnessing the annual performance, in a Caribbean village,
of scenes from the *Ramayana* enacted by the descendants
of indentured cane cutters from India. Lalbihari Sharma is
a far less celebrated, utterly obscure source. But how won-
derful is this text—what a magical find! A pleasure to read
him across this distance of time in Rajiv Mohabir's clear
translation. Over the heartbreak of displacement and loss,
what I hear, as if delivered to the accompaniment of a dhol
and majira, is an energetic recitation: the mixed rhythm
of faith and a newfound feeling of identity particular to
the Caribbean."
—Amitava Kumar, author of *Immigrant, Montana*

"Much has been written about the people who were
brought—at the end of the 19th and into the early 20th cen-
turies—to the British West Indian colonies to work the cane
fields, but the voices of the workers themselves have been
either silent or imagined by theorists and by their yearning
ancestors. And if we do hear from them, it has until now
usually been about their very real tribulations as indentured
laborers. Rajiv Mohabir's important translation of Lalbihari

Sharma's poems, a literary expression that will challenge and alter our preconceptions of the early Indian worker in the Caribbean, is a rare and important glimpse into the life and mind of a man whose voice soars well above the position of laborer in someone else's service. The cane field is and is not present in these poems, it is not the whole, the laborer is an individual, a learned person, humanist, poet, lover, and dreamer; he is undefeated because of creativity and the richness of his mind. Mohabir's essay on how he himself came to poetry and to this work by Sharma is itself an enlightening and delightful revelation. Thank you, Rajiv, for this beautiful service to our past, and to our future."
—Shani Mootoo, author of *Moving Forward Sideways Like a Crab*

"This is an extraordinary text. Penned in British Guiana by a former indentured laborer from Northern India who became an overseer and then a landowner, these verses and religious songs hold within them a rich and complex account of the struggles, separations, and longings of indentured Indians in the Caribbean. As the only known work of its kind, the text is of tremendous historical significance. But equally significant is the process by which this sheaf of verses has come to publication in English: pursued by the writer and historian Gaiutra Bahadur; rescued from a mislabeled folder by an archivist; deciphered by an itinerant reader of religious texts in Trinidad and an Indian American scholar in Ohio; and finally brought into English verse by the Indo-Caribbean American poet, scholar, and translator Rajiv Mohabir. *I Even Regret Night* contains a multitude of migrant lives and voices that resonate across oceans and across time."
—Vivek Bald, author of *Bengali Harlem and the Lost History of South Asian America*

"Lalbihari Sharma claims to have created this collection, "for the joy of music lovers and to purify myself"; the translator, a descendent from this tradition, recreates these spiritual songs with inspired verse that continues to sing for us in English. A scholarly essay included in this collection provides much needed context, while the direct, honed lines often approach the inspiration and purification of prayer."
—Roger Sedarat, Queens College

"What a fortune! What a tragedy! From the ache of indenture rises this century-old manuscript, in a stunning bilingual edition adorned with images from the plantation. Rajiv Mohabir's sensitive translation, along with the Afterword by scholar-author Gaiutra Bahadur that beautifully contextualizes it, breathes a whole new lifetime into these poems. The verses poignantly document life for the entrapped workers—"bearing hoes on their shoulders" at 5 am, the sahib bearing a whip, years passing "in steady woe." They also introduce English readers to new (to us) forms—from up-tempo odes celebrating the divine festival to dirges mourning a lost homeland—that sing out like an absent lover. This treasure establishes Lalbihari Sharma as the southernmost star in the firmament of bhakti poets, and Mohabir in the ranks of esteemed translators such as Bly and Barks who have brought the mystic lover-poets of South Asia into our English."

—Minal Hajratwala, author of *Leaving India: My Family's Journey from Five Villages to Five Continents*

"A suddenly recovered world of American spiritual folksong opens up here in these celebrations by Lalbihari Sharma. Mohabir's 'chutney' translations make the loss, longing, and hope sting again. It is as though Guyana's cane plantations always harbored India's gods of the dispossessed. Here is Kabir's tradition, here Mirabai's, but native to the soil of the Americas: pungent, salty, hopeful, quick. These songs make your hair stand up. Mohabir gives them with a stirring account of translation as family-discovery. Gaiutra Bahadur, in a sharp essay, tells of the near-miracle of finding a lost manuscript, and with it, an all but lost history."

—Andrew Schelling, translator of *Bright as an Autumn Moon: Fifty Poems from the Sanskrit*

I Even Regret Night

Holi Songs of Demerara

I Even Regret Night
Holi Songs of Demerara

Lalbihari Sharma
Translated by Rajiv Mohabir

KAYA PRESS | Los Angeles • New York

22 21 20 19 4 3 2 1

Published by Kaya Press
www.Kaya.com

Cover illustration by Nisha Sethi
Cover and book design by Ziyi Xu

Distributed by D.A.P./Distributed Art Publishers
75 Broad Street Suite 630 New York, NY 10004
800.338.BOOK   www.artbook.com

ISBN: 9781885030597

Library of Congress Control Number: 2018961925
Sharma, Lalbihari . Transl. Mohabir, Rajiv.
I Even Regret Night: Holi Songs of Demerara

Printed in the United States of America

This publication is made possible by support from the USC Dana
and David Dornsife College of Arts, Letters, and Sciences; the
Shinso Ito Center for Japanese Religions and Culture; and the USC
Department of American Studies and Ethnicity. Special thanks
to the Choi Chang Soo Foundation for their support of this work.
Additional funding was provided by the generous contributions
of: Christine Alberto, Tiffany Babb, Manibha Banerjee, Tom and
Lily So Beischer, Piyali Bhattacharya, Jade Chang, Anelise Chen,
Anita Chen, Lisa Chen, Floyd Cheung, Jen Chou, Kavita Das, Steven
Doi, Susannah Donahue, Jessica Eng, Sesshu Foster, Jean Ho,
Heidi Hong, Huy Hong, Jayson Joseph, Sabrina Ko, Juliana Koo,
Whakyung Lee, Andrew Leong, Edward Lin, Leza Lowitz, Edan
Lepucki, Faisal Mohyuddin, Nayomi Munaweera, Abir Majumdar,
Viet Thanh Nguyen, Sandra Noel, Chez Bryan Ong, Gene & Sabine
Oishi, Leena Pendharker, Eming Piansay, Amarnath Ravva, Andrew
Shih, Paul H. Smith, Shinae Yoon, Monona Wali, Patricia Wakida,
Duncan Williams, Amelia Wu & Sachin Adarkar, Anita Wu & James
Spicer, Koon Woon, Mikoto Yoshida, Nancy Yap, and others.

Kaya Press is also supported, in part, by the National Endowment
for the Arts; the Los Angeles County Board of Supervisors through
the Los Angeles County Arts Commission; the City of Los Angeles
Department of Cultural Affairs; and the Community of Literary
Magazines and Presses.

For the descendants of Lalbihari Sharma;
For all the descendants of indenture—

Table Of Contents

Introduction
Rajiv Mohabir, Translator

Imagine you are in a cane field far from home. Somewhere in the distance, the familiar beat of a dholak drum, the familiar whine of a poem sung half in Braj Bhasha and half in Bhojpuri. Your pagri is heavy with sweat from midday work. You untie the cloth from your head and sit down. You hear narrated within earshot the trials that arise from life as an indentured laborer on a sugar plantation. Today your bundles of cane stalk will be counted. The jill you earn you may decide to ferret away for some later date, or you may use it to buy rum at the local shop. The year is 1916. You are in Demerara, British Guyana.[1] A formerly indentured man named Lalbihari Sharma has just published a book of songs that are to be sung during the month of Phagun.

Phagun is the month of the festival of colors, of Phagua in the Bhojpuri language or Holi in Hindi.[2] This is a time when the devout celebrate the triumph of devotion over ignorance and the rebirth of the earth after the death of winter. On the morning of Holi, Hindus, Muslims, and Christians all rejoice by throwing colors and visiting people in their communities. Here in Guyana, people sing and play up-tempo music in celebration. The phaags they sing bring joy and help alleviate the misery of bondage. They remind you of comfort, of home, of the gods. They remind you that this suffering is temporary.

Your plan is to return to India after serving out your five-year contract, but the reality is that you will never go back. The promise of return will never be fulfilled, and your children, grandchildren, and great-great-grandchildren will feel the hollow of this reneged promise. The cane you cut today will continue its leafy bite for generations of dispossession. But for now, listen to the music. Imagine you are able to escape the horrors of not having enough to eat, of being thought of as less than human by those who bind you and your family members to their contracts. Imagine your soul is a bird that will one day fly from its cage.

◆●●━━

[1] The colony of British Guiana became the independent nation of Guyana in 1966. Throughout the book, spellings will shift depending on context.

[2] Holi is a celebration of the devotion of Prince Prahlad, who proves his dedication to the Divine when he refuses his father, the wicked king Hirnayakashipu, who has demanded his worship. At the orders of the king, the less devout Princess Holika, Prahlad's sister, holds her wayward brother in a fire, burning up the night, then burning up herself when the Lord comes to earth in the shape of Narsingh-dev—half man, half lion—to rip out the king's intestines and protect Prahlad, who had tirelessly chanted the name of god during his ordeal.

TRANSLATOR'S NOTE: Throughout this collection, there are multiple words that the poet uses to address the beloved. Following bhakti poetic tradition, he assumes at different points the voices of Radha and Sita, incarnations of the goddess Lakshmi and consorts to incarnations of Vishnu. At times, the speaker cries out *piya*, echoing the koyal bird, which sings a song that sounds like a lament in the rainy season. At other times, the speaker invokes the name Hari—an epithet for Vishnu as well as for Rama and Krishna, the seventh and eighth incarnations of Vishnu—in Puranic Hinduism. Sharma also employs the voice of the lover, which is almost always womanly, as she speaks to her friends and women kinfolk, whom she refers to as "sakhi" or "sakhiya."

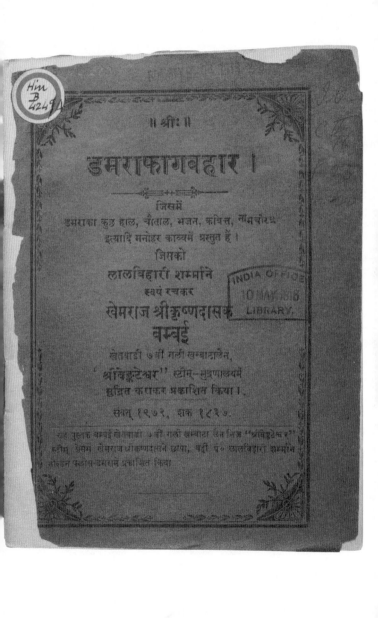

॥ श्रीः ॥

डमराका फागवहार ।

जिसमें

डमराका कुछ हाल, चैताल, भजन, कवित्त, नौबतोरा

इत्यादि मनोहर काव्यमें प्रस्तुत हें ।

जिसको

लालबिहारी शर्माने

स्वयं रचकर

खेमराज श्रीकृष्णदासके

बम्बई

खेतवाडी ७ वीं गली खम्बाटालेन,

"श्रीवेङ्कटेश्वर" स्टीम्-मुद्रणालयमें

मुद्रित कराकर प्रकाशित किया ।

संवत् १९७२, शाक १८३७ ।

यह पुस्तक बम्बई खेतवाडी ७ वीं गली कन्नादा लेन निज "श्रीवेङ्कटेश्वर" स्टीम् प्रेसमे खेमराज श्रीकृष्णदासने छापा, बडी प० लालबिहारी शर्माने और डन फागोश डमरासे प्रकाशित किया

20 | Sharma', La'lbiha'ri.—डमरा फाग बहार. [Damrá Fág Bahár. Fag or Holi songs of Damrá. A collection of songs meant to be sung during the celebration of the Holi Festival.] pp. 34. Published by the author, Damerasa. Samvat 1972. [11th Feb. 1916.] Super Royal 16mo. 1st edition.

Price. As. 1-6.

Holi Songs of Demerara

सूचना

यह पुस्तक मैंने गायनप्रिय रसिकोंके आनन्दार्थ तथा अपना अन्त:करण पवित्र करनेके लिये बनाया है इसमें कुछएक डमराकी व्यवस्था, चौताल, भजन, कबित्त इत्यादि छंदोंमें बिबिध कथाप्रसंग वर्णन कियाहै। यदि रसिकजन इसे पढकर पावें तो मैं अपने परिश्रमको सफल समझूंगा, उपसंहारमें सर्ब सह्रदय महोदयोंसे सबिनय निबेदन है कि इस ग्रन्थमें रहेहुए प्रमादोंको कृपाके साथ क्षमा करैं।

लालबिहारीशर्मा,
गोलडेनफ्लीस,
डमरा.

Preface

I have created this book of playful songs for the joy
of music lovers and to purify myself; in these pages I
have collected various songs such as chautal, bhajan,
kavitt, and other miscellaneous types. If music lovers
should read this and derive some pleasure then I will
consider my work successful. Finally, if you should
find any mistakes or unwarranted joy where it is
misplaced, please forgive me.

Lalbihari Sharma
Golden Fleece
Damra

Invocation
वन्दना

अथ डमराफागबहारप्रारम्भ।

वन्दना
चौपाई

वन्दों रामचरण सुभकारी।
सहित कमलपद जनकदुलारी ॥ १ ॥

सुमिरों शिव गिरिराजकुमारी।
करहु कृपा मोहिं जानि दुखारी ॥ २ ॥

गो गणेशके चरण मनाऊँ।
जिनकी कृपा स्वच्छ मति पाऊँ ॥ ३ ॥

प्रणवों महावीर हनुमान।
निशिदिन धरो चरणपर ध्याना ॥ ४ ॥

सूर्यनरायण इष्ट हमारे।
सुमिरत जाहि मिटैं दुख भारे ॥ ५ ॥

श्रीगुरुपदकी रज धरि माथा।
पूरण करन चहों यह गाथा ॥ ६ ॥

Invocation
Chaupai

At Rama's feet I bow, bringer of auspice;
I bow before Janak's beloved daughter.

Shiva and Parvati, the mountain princess,
expel my sadness.

The elephant-headed god's feet,
have grace to cleanse my thoughts.

Pranam to the great warrior Hanuman,
I meditate night and day on your feet.

Surya, my lord, to whom I am devoted,
reflecting on you, all sorrows flee.

I touch my head to the dust of the Guru's feet,
bless the completion of my epic.

दोहा

लालबिहारी कर बिनय, सुनिये सन्त सुजान॥
मेरे मनकी कामना, सिद्ध करे भगवान॥१॥

संत समागम सुलभ अति, करहु सदा चित लाइ॥
अंतसमय सुख होत है, ममता मल जरि जाइ॥२॥

मोहिं भरोसा रामका, राखतहीं विश्वास॥
प्रणतारत हर नाम जिहि, हरिहैं सो मम त्रास॥३॥

Doha

Lalbihari asks, "Saints and wise-folk alike,
      hear this. May the devas fulfill
my desires. Where saints gather,
      raise your hands. At the end

may you find bliss, departing this world
      of rapture and shit. Believe me,
I trust Rama. Of all the names you recite,
      what awe is greater than Hari."

The Tale Of Demerara
निजबयान सहित डमराका बयान

छंद

भूमिजन्मका प्रान्त छपरागांव मैरीटांड़हैं ॥

ब्रह्मदेवकर पुत्र जानो,
लालविहारी नाम है ॥

आइके हम बास कीन्हां,
देश डमरालोक है ॥

रहत हम हैं शरणप्रभुके ।
कटत दिन सब नीकहै ॥ १ ॥

Chand

In the region of his birth,
    in Chhapra district in Mairitaand village,

Lord Brahma begat a son
    named Lalbihari, the Beloved of Bihar.

Having come here, I live in the country
    of Demerara. I pass my days

in the refuge that is Hari.

दोहा

बृटिस गयाना देशमें, यद्यपि प्रांत अनेक ॥
कहुं विचित्र कहुँ अतिदुखी, यहनिज मनकर टेक ॥ १ ॥

ऐस्सीकुइबो प्रांतमें, गोल्डनफ्लीस एक गांव ॥
अति सुन्दर अस्थान यह, सब जानत यह ठांव ॥ २ ॥

पंडित परमानन्दजी, बासी जहंकर आहि ॥
सबहीको वह बिदितहै, देश विदेशन माहिं ॥ ३ ॥

रामचरण पुनि बंदिकर, महिसुरपद मन धार ॥
पंडितजीके चरण युग, हमरे प्राण अधार ॥ ४ ॥

Doha

There are many provinces in British Guiana:
some queer, some miserable, depending

on your own eyes. Everyone knows
the wondrous village of

Golden Fleece in Essiquibo District.
Where Pandit Paramanand resides

is renowned both here and abroad.
Again I bow before Rama; also I bow

before the wise one's feet,
the foundation of my life.

Demerara's Condition
डमराका हाल

चौपाई

लिखन चहों कुछ डमरारीती । सुनिहैं सज्जन करि प्रीती ॥
यह है देश कुदेश अपारा । रहत न धर्म विवेक विचारा ॥
देश छाँड़िकर डमरा आय । आपन नाम सो कुली लिखाय ॥
भजन छाँड़ि छाँड़े निजधरमा । छाँड़ि वेदपथ करहिं कुकरमा ॥
नित्यकर्म जो डमरामाहीं । सो अब लिखों कबित्तके माहीं ॥

Chaupai

I want to write a little
    of Demerara's customs. Listen,
this is a country of infinite ills,
    where wisdom is scarce.

I left my home and came to Demerara,
    my name penned as "Coolie."
Forsaking bhajans, forsaking dharma,
    the Vedas I abandoned, to my disgrace.

Of the routines of this Demerara life,
    I write these kavitt, these verses.

कवित्त

बाजी घंटी पांचकी कि हण्डी दीनी है चढाय,
भात लियाहै बनाय दही चीनी मेलिके।

खायके अनन्द भये द्वारे आये सरदार,
ठाढे करत पुकार आग्यदें सम्हारके।

अब धोयके ससपान भात लेतहैं भराय,
चीलम तयार करि धरत सम्हारके।

जमा भये नर नारि कान्धे धरेहैंकुदारि,
भीर भइ भारी पहुँचे डमरहु जायके॥

Kavitt

As the bell tolls five, the pot heats
    on the fire: rice and yogurt boil
with sugar. I eat my fill and
    the sardar comes to the door,
bringing orders we must endure.
    Washing the pot I keep the rice,
I prepare my chillam pipe to deal
    with this. Men and women join together
bearing hoes on their shoulders,
    the way clogged with those
who have come to Demerara.

डमराका हाल

पहिले पानीमें हेलाय लत्ताकपड़ाकी
भिजाय आयेहैं सरदार काम देतहै बतायके॥

Demerara's Condition

First we ford the waterway,
our ragged clothes soaked.

The sardar comes
to apportion our tasks.

दोहा

ता पाछे साहेब चला, टोपी ऊंच लगाय ॥
चाबुक लीन्हो हाथमें, सरपट पहुँचा आय ॥

Doha

Then behind us comes the sahib,
hat high on his head.

Grasping a whip, horse
cantering, he reaches the field.

कवित्त

बुक लीयोहै निकाल पहुँचा कुलियोंमें जाय,
काम लिखत बनाय सब देख देखके ॥

जाकर है काम खोटो ताकर पैसा लीन्हो काटि,
करत खराब मेरी काया काँपै देखिके ॥

डमरा टापु बरजोर पुलीस थाना चहुंओर,
राम कहां लायेहो गरीबन भुलायके ॥

Kavitt

Bearing a book, the sardar reaches
    the coolies. Inspecting the cane field,
he accounts their work. If one does not finish
    the tasks, he vexes, then garnishes pay.
When I witness this my entire body shakes.
    In Demerara there are police
stations in every direction. O god, where
    have they taken and forgotten the poor?

दोहा

आये सनीचर रंगला, खुसी भईं नर नारि ॥
ओढ़े पंचरँगचुनरी, चलि मंजा दरबारि ॥

Doha

Come Saturday, men
and women finally make merry.

Covered with orhnis,
scarves of five hues,

they approach
the manager's court.

कवित्त

कोई पहिर बाजूबन्द कोई खडीहैं दुकन्ध,
काजर मनोहर नयनोंसे लगायके ॥

आये सरदार करि काज सबके सम्हार,
पयसा देत नर नारि सबन देवायके ॥

Kavitt

Some in armbands, some standing,
    their lovely waterlines besmeared in kohl.
When the sardar comes, he attends to all matters,
    giving men and women their money.

चौपाई

बीते पांच बरिस यहिभांती ॥
चिन्ता सोक करत दिनराती ॥

टिकट पाइ मन भयउ अनन्दा ॥

जिमि चकोरसिसु निरखत चन्दा ॥
भयउ प्रमोद धरहि नहिं धीरा ॥

कोइ साधु कोइ बने फकीरा ॥

होइ अधीर चहूँदिसि धावहिं ॥
एको जुक्ति न मनमें लावहिं ॥

Chaupai

In this manner five years pass
    in steady woe. With a ticket,
the heart, like a chakor bird,
    cries out to the moon.

Such mirth! Some act as sadhus,
    some fakirs, wildly
prancing all around, without any idea
    of what comes next.

दोहा

सौमें एक धीरज धरी, रहे गांवके माहिं॥
बात सुने सरदारके, खुसी रहें मनमाहिं॥

Doha

One out of one hundred are patient
as before in the village.

If they obey the sardar,
their hearts remain content.

The Work of Poet Lalbihari Sharma in Chautal

ताल चौताल डमरैला
कवि लालबिहारी शर्मा कृत

डमराफागबहार

रौरे चरननके बलिहारि बिदेहकुमारी ॥

सुन नर मुनि सब ध्यान धरत हैं नाम जपत त्रिपुरारी ॥
लख चौरासी जीव जगतमें, हो सिर नावत चरन तुमारी ॥ १॥
अपने इच्छा प्रगट भयी तुम जस छाये संसारी ॥
लीला जो कीन जनकपुरके महँ, तुम मोहिलियो नर नारी ॥ २॥
पूजन हेतु चली बगियामें, झुण्ड सखिनकी भारी ॥
गावत गीत मनोहर बानी हो, तहां राम मिले फुलवारी ॥ ३॥
फूलन काज गये रघुनन्दन, मिलिगइ जनकदुलारी ॥
प्रीति परसपर केहिबिधि बरनों, तुमरे सरनमें लालबिहारी ॥ ४॥

Invocation

From your feet: the devotee, Sita.

Gods, men, seers, all beings
meditate on Shiva's name.
One million and eighty-four species

in this world bow at your feet.
Your desire is clear,
your celebrity paints its shadow

on the world. As in Janakpur,
you enchant men and women.
To perform puja, Sita went to the garden

filled with jhandi flags. Singing,
she met Lord Rama amidst the blooms.
The prince, gathering flowers,

met Janak's beloved daughter.
How to speak of such love?
Lalbihari seeks shelter at your feet.

उलारा

सोह नवल तनु सुन्दर सारी ॥
सोह नवल तनु सुन्दर सारी ॥
देस देसके राजा मोहे,
देस देसके राजा मोहे ॥
मोहत सब नर नारी,
सोह नचल तनु सुन्दर सारी ॥

Ulara

She stuns. Her beauty,
unique, bewitches kings
the world over, captures
the hearts of men
and women.

चौताल

जननी जगतारनहारी महेस पियारी ॥
महिषासुरके प्राण लियो तुम, सुंभ निसुंभ पछारी ॥

जाइ पताल हती अहिरावण,
तहां असुरके झुण्ड बिदारी ॥ १ ॥

रक्तबीजबध कारण माता, काली रूप सवांरी ॥

सकल भुवनकर जीभ बनाइहो,
सब राक्षस यहि बिधि मारी ॥ २ ॥

आइ बास पाटनमें कीन्हो, देव सुमनझरि डारी ॥

अक्षत चन्दन बेलके पाती हो,
तहां पूजन होत तुम्हारी ॥ ३ ॥

लालबिहारी बिनै यह गावत जय जय शब्द उचारी ॥

बेदबिदित तुम्हरो जस बरणत,
तुम दीननके हितकारी ॥ ४ ॥

Chautal

Ma, redeemer, Shiva's beloved,
you served the buffalo-demon
Mahishasur his last breath.
To kill Ahiravan you descend

to Pataal and slay droves
of asuras like the beast Raktabij.
You take Kali's form. With
the universe on your tongue

you destroy every rakshas.
You dwell in Patan, where
the gods' flowers cascade about you,
where, with sandalwood

and bel leaves, people worship you.
Even without Lalbihari the words
"Victory! Victory!" ring out. The Vedas recount
your glory, your support of the helpless.

उलारा

जै गजबदन षड़ानन माता ॥
जै गजबदन षड़ानन माता ॥
सुर नर मुनि सब ध्यान धरतहैं,
सुर नर मुनि सब ध्यान धरतहैं ॥
संकर प्रिय तुम सब सुख दाता,
जै गजबदन षड़ानन माता ॥

Ulara

Praise to the mother whose body
bore Ganesh. Glory to Parvati.
Gods, men, seers all meditate on you,
beloved of Shiva-Shankar,
giver of joy. Victory to
you, goddess, mother
of the elephant-headed one.

चौताल

शिवसंकर खेलत होरी समाज बनाई॥
डिमकि डिमकि डमरू कर बाजत तननन भृंगी बजाई॥

सररर सररर सृंगी बाजत,
जहां सरगम भेद बताई॥१॥

ताक धिनाधिन ताक धिनाधिन ताक धिनाधिन ताहो॥

धुधुकट धुधुकट धुधुकट धुधुकट
यहीभाँति मृदंग बजाई॥२॥

झननन झननन नचे योगिनी भूत प्रेत संग लाई,

फररर फररर चलत धरणिपर,
जहां सननन श्रवण सुनाई॥३॥

Chautal

Shiva-Shankar makes a people play Holi.

Dimki dimki
on the damaru drum;
tananana plays the bhriġi.

Sararara sararara
the bowed sarangi lilts
the solfa,

Tak dhinadhin
    tak dhinadhin
        tak dhinadhin
            taho.

Dhudhukat
    dhudhukat
        dhudhukat
            dhudhukat

beats the mridang drum.

Jhananana jhananana
dances the yoġini
with ghosts and spirits.

Phararara phararara
she walks the beam where
sananana rings out.

Chapat chapat
beats the tapori,

चटपट चटपट बजे थपोरी अनहद शब्द सुनाई,

लालबिहारी कहत हर हर हर,
तहां अबिर गुलाल उड़ाई ॥४॥

in countless words Lalbihari chants,

letting colors fly.

उलारा

शिव शिव जपत सो मन आनन्दा,
शिव शिव जपत सो मन आनन्दा ॥
आदिदेव संकर कहं जानो,
आदिदेव संकर कहं जानो ॥
अंग भभूत भालपर चन्दा,
शिव शिव जपत सो मन आनन्दा ॥

Ulara

Chant *Shiva-Shiva*
and get lost in ecstasy.

Shankar is first amongst
the gods, principal amongst devas.

Body smeared with ash,
the moon crowns his head.

Chant *Shiva-Shiva*
and lose yourself.

चौताल

मुनिसंग चले दोउ भाइ मनहि हर्षाई ॥
बगसरजाइ ताड़का मारे मुनिकर यग्य कराई ॥

गौतमनारि अहिल्या तारी,
तहां मुनिकर स्राप छोड़ाई ॥ १ ॥

कौशिक कहें अहो नृपबालक सुनो बात मन लाई,

तिरहुतराज परण एक कीन्हो,
शिव संकर धनुष धराई ॥ २ ॥

सो सीतासंग ब्याहे जइहैं जो यह धनुष चढ़ाई,

देस देसके भूपति आयेहो,
तहां रावण बाण लजाई ॥ ३ ॥

उठे राम गुरु आयसु लैके धन्वा दीन्ह चढ़ाई ॥

लालबिहारी कहत भंजउ,
तब जनकसुता बरि पाई ॥ ४ ।

Chautal

Rama and Lakshman embark,
joyful, to slay the demon Tardka
so the seers could perform
Vedic ritual unmolested. They free

Gautam's wife, Ahilya, of a curse
that turned her body to stone.
Kaushik says, "O Princes, listen.
The King of Mithila swears

he who lifts and strings Shiva's
immovable bow will marry Sita."
Kings came from afar;
there Ravan was shamed.

Up rose Rama with the Guru's
blessings to string Shankar's bow.

              Lalbihari says, "The bow
strung; Janak's daughter won."

उलारा

राम लषण दसरथके ढाटा,
राम लषण दसरथके ढाटा॥
परसराम तहं देखि चकित भये,
परसराम तहं देखि चकित भये॥
बाल मरालनके कल जोटा,
राम लषण दसरथके ढाटा॥

Ulara

Rama and Lakshman, sons
of the Raghu line, shocked
Parashuram with their greatness.
The sons of Awadh, Rama
and Lakshman, dazzled
Parashuram with their might.

चौताल

सीया मति करु बदन मलीन राम बर पाय ॥
करि सिंगार सखिनके संगमें चलिभइ जनककी जाय ॥

पहुंची बाग सकल दिसि चितवत,
सखी राम लषण मन भाय ॥ १ ॥

बोलन चहति बात नहिं आवत देखि सखिन सकुचाय,

गौरीपूजन मनमें धरिकेहो,
तहां भंवर रहे मुखछाय ॥ २ ॥

देखि सियामुख राम लोभायत नेक धीर नहिं आय ॥

सियमुख ससिभये नयन चहोराहो,
तहां सखिन रहीं ललचाय ॥ ३ ॥

लेकर फूल चले दोउ भाई चलत समय पछिताय ॥

लालबिहारी कहत कर जोरीहो,
मोरे रामचरण मन भाय ॥ ४ ॥

Chautal

The bright Sita gained Rama's dark body
as a husband. Adorned in jewels,
her friends sent her off
to the garden to distract her,

Rama and Lakshman's hearts
now hers. Sita opened
her mouth but no sound came out.
Looking around, she saw her friends

and blushed. Praying to the goddess,
her face flushed. Beholding Sita,
Rama's stalwart heart stirred.
Sita's face like the moon, Rama's eyes

like chakor birds, there in the garden.
Sita's friends burned with jealousy.
Bringing flowers, the brothers depart.

Lalbihari says, "Rama's feet won my heart."

उलारा

रघुबंसिनकर सहज सुभाऊ,
रघुबंसिनकर सहज सुभाऊ ॥
कहतानि राम लषणसे बतिया,
कहतानि राम लषणसे बतिया ॥
मन कुपंथ मग धरे न काऊ,
रघुबंसिनकर सहज सुभाऊ ॥

Ulara

Raghu dynasty's scion
says with wit—
Rama to Lakshman—
"May you never stray
from the righteous path."

चौताल

अब दसरथ राज कुमार खेलें सब होरी ॥
राम लच्छमन भरत सत्रुहन हाथ लिये पिचकारी ॥

तेहि बिच सोभित जनकदुलारीहो,
तनु पाट पीतम्बर सारी ॥ १ ॥

ढोल मृदंग झांझ बहु बाजत भीर भई अतिभारी ॥

उड़त अबीर लाल भये बादर,
तहां छीपिगयेहैं तमारी ॥ २ ॥

खेलत फाग परसपर हिलिमिलि देव सुमन झरि डारी ॥

परम अनन्द अवध नरनारीहो,
तहां जयजय शब्द पुकारी ॥ ३ ॥

ब्रह्मा बिष्णु देव सब आये उमा सहित त्रिपुरारी ॥

अस्तुति करि निजलोक सिधाय हो,
उनके सरणमें लालबिहारी ॥ ४ ॥

Chautal

Now all Dasharath's sons play Holi.
Rama, Lakshman, Bharat, and
Sathruhan's, whose hands bear pichkari guns.
Between them, Janak's beloved daughter

glows, clad in her yellow sari.
Beat the dhol, mridang, jhanjh drums
and call the crowd. The abir flies
until its red cloud hides

all darkness. Everyone together
plays Holi; the gods shower flowers.
Enraptured men and women
of Awadh cry out, *Jai! Jai!*

Brahma, Vishnu—all devas gather.
With Uma came Shiva. After singing
their praises, Lalbihari returns
to his world in their shelter.

उलारा

जबसे राम ब्याहि घर आये,
जबसे राम ब्याहि घर आये ॥
खेलत फाग अवधमें भारी,
खेलत फाग अवधमें भारी ॥
नित नवमंगल मोद बधाये,
जबसे राम ब्याहि घर आये ॥

Ulara

Rama married;
since his return,
he throws Holi colors
in Awadh. Who is not
ecstatic, dancing madly,
since the prince returned
wed?

चौताल

श्रीबरणहु सब मुनि देव बिबेक बिचारी ।
ब्रह्मा बिष्णु महेस अरु नारद, राम कृष्ण तनु धारी ॥

वरुण कुबेर सुरुज अरु चन्दाहो,
तहां सारद सब हितकारी ॥ १ ॥

पारबतीके चरण मनाऊं गननायक महतारी ॥

इन्द्र प्रबल सब देवके राजहो,
बीच राजित जनक दुलारी ॥ २ ॥

गुरु भृगुनायक सनक सनन्दन और देवमुनि झारी ॥

गाधिसुवन तहां सहित बसिष्ठहो,
तहां कुम्भज मुनि गुणभारी ॥ ३ ॥

बावन बौध कलंकी जानो कच्छ मच्छ नरहारी ॥

परसराम बराह बखानत,
सबके सरणमें लालबिहारी ॥ ४ ॥

Chautal

I think now of every saint and deva
with clear wisdom. Brahma, Vishnu,
Shiva, and the saint Narad.
Rama and Krishna. Varun, Kuber,

Sun and Moon, where there is favor.
At the feet of Parvati,
I sing to the mighty Indra, king
of the gods, and to Sita,

Janak's beloved daughter.
Guru Bhriganayak, Sanak, Sananadan.
The devas and munis gather, too.
Gadhisuwan escorts Vashishta,

honorable Kumbhaj comes, too.
More than fifty wise and sinful born
assemble, Parasuram accounts
for all. At his feet sits Lalbihari.

उलारा

देवनेक अब बिनय सुनाऊ,
देवनेक अब बिनय सुनाऊं ॥
मोर मनोरथ पुरवहु हियके,
मोर मनोरथ पुरवहु हियके ॥
जिनके कृपा निरमल मति पाऊं
देवनेक अब बिनय सुनाऊं ॥

Ulara

Now to the gods
I humbly sing—
May my heart's desire
be granted;
my want
fulfilled.

चौताल

अब लिखन चहौं कुछ हाल सुनो धरि ध्याना ॥
गर्भबासमें जब तुम आये याद भये भगवाना ॥

जन्म भये तब रोवनलगे हो,
तहां घेरिलीय मदमाना ॥ १ ॥

बालापन लडिकन संग खेले भूलिगये हरि ध्याना ॥

जवानभये तिरियन संग रीझत,
तब चाल चलतहैं उताना ॥ २ ॥

कारी गई सपेती आई चमड़ा लाग सुखाना ॥

आंखके अंधा कानके बहिराहो,
अब दांतन भयहैं निदाना ॥ ३ ॥

उमिरि बिताये मोहजालमें काल गये निगिचाना ॥

लालबिहारी कहत समुझाइहो,
भजु मायापति भगवाना ॥ ४ ॥

Chautal

Now attend what I write.
Since the womb, you've thought
of god. Weeping at birth
you were surrounded by rejoicing.

During childhood, playing with friends,
you forgot Hari. And in youth
you fell into love's foolish haze.
Time passed and your skin

began its drying wilt. Eyes blind,
ears deaf, your teeth have all fallen out.
You spent your life seduced
by the web of senses and time

and passed through this world
of maya, of illusion.

        Lalbihari says
so you understand, "Think of god,
the lord of illusion."

उलारा

आखिर झूठ जगतहै सपना,
आखिर झूठ जगतहै सपना ॥
धन दवलत परिवार बड़ाई,
धर दवलत परिवार बड़ाई ॥
यह सब माया नहिं है अपना,
आखिर झूठ जगतहै सपना ॥

Ulara

In the end, this world is a sham,
a dream, a lie:
wealth, family, greatness,
riches, kinship, fame—
all illusory.

None of it is yours.

चौताल

सखी फूले बसन्तके फूल बिरह तनु जारे ॥
चम्पा फुले गुलाब फुलाने सुरुजमुखी कचनारे ॥

उड़हुल बेलि चमेलि फुलानेहो,
सर कमल फुले रतनारे ॥ १ ॥

जुही मालती कंदइल दाड़िम गोंदा फुले हजारे ॥

लाल अनार कुसुमकलियनहो
सखी सिरीस फुले अति बारे ॥ २ ॥

बाग पियाबिन फूल फुलाने मारत जान हमारे ॥

जो पीया होत हमारे संगमेंहो,
सखि करत बिथा सब न्यारे ॥ ३ ॥

कोइल सब्द करत बगियामें सुनि सुनि फटत दरारे ॥

लालबिहारी कहत समुझाइ हो,
गोरी तुमरो बलम अतिबारे ॥ ४ ॥

Chautal

Even with spring's blossoms
unfolding, separation stings.
Frangipani, roses, sunflowers,
hibiscus, and jasmine unfurl

as night folds. Juhi and honeysuckle
erupt as flames—
thousands of match-like marigolds.
The red pomegranate buds,

the silk flower in fine bloom.
In the garden, without my beloved,
flowers slay me. O friends,
O sakhi, were he beside me,

he'd banish my fears. In the garden
the koyal's each cry breaks me.

Lalbihari explains, "Fair one,
your beloved soon comes."

उलारा

गुल्लनारेमें राधा प्यारी बसे,
गुल्लनारेमें राधा प्यारी बसे ॥
फुलवा महँकरहे बगियामें,
फुलवा महँकरहे बगियामें ॥
महँक रहे बगियामें ॥
सखि जाहीजुहीमें कन्हैया बसे
गुल्लनारेमें राधा प्यारी बसे ॥

Ulara

In the pomegranate flower
Radha dwells.

O sakhi,
in the jasmine,
Krishna.

Radha dances
in the fire-
bloom.

चौताल

पपीहा बन बैन सुनावे नींद नहीं आवे ॥
आधीरात भई जब सखिया कामबिरह सन्तावे ॥

पियबिन चैन मनहि नहिं आवत,
सखि जोबन जोर जनावे ॥१॥

फागुन मस्त महीना सजनी पियबिन मोहिं न भावे ॥

पवन झकोरत लुह जनु लागत,
गोरी बैठी तहां पछितावे ॥२॥

सब सखि मिलकर फाग रचतहैं । ढोल मृदंग बजावे ॥

हाथ अबीर कनक पिचकारी हो,
सखि देखत मन दुख पावे ॥३॥

हे बिधना मैं काह बिगाड़ो जनम अकारथ जावे ॥

लालबिहारी कहत समुझाइ हो,
गोरी धीरजमें सुख पावे ॥४॥

Chautal

In the forest, the papiha bird's epics
stave off sleep. It's at midnight
separation from my love
torments me. Without him

I have no peace. My youth wastes.
Phagun is supposed to be a blissful month,
but without Krishna, how can
I enjoy it? Should the day-breeze blow,

it's blistering. I even regret night.
All my friends gather to compose
chautal songs, knocking drums.
Abir in the hands and colored water;

my pain wakes. What fate
that I take such a ruinous life
and squander it.

           Lalbihari says, "Fair one,
with peace comes happiness."

उलारा

भतरा मोर दढिजराके नाती,
भतरा मोर दढिजराके नाती ॥
मैं जो बोलों तबहुँ न बोले,
मैं जो बोलों तबहुँ न बोले ॥
आनके देखि चले अठलाती,
भतरा मोर दढ़िजराके नाती ॥

Ulara

My love, do not vex.
What I say
and what I don't say
is only what I've seen.
What use is anger?

चौताल

सखि उठिकर करहु सिंगार बसन्त जाये ॥
बाजुबन्द कंगन भल सोहे अँगुरिन नेपुर भाय ॥

पहिरि बिजायठ हार जो सोहत,
सिर बेन्दी मन लाय ॥१॥

करि सिंगार पलंगपर बैठी पिया पिया गोहराय ॥

मैं बिरहिनि पिया बात न पूछत,
तब जोबन जोर जनाय ॥२॥

चोलिया मसके बन्द सब टूटे अंग अंग थहराय ॥

कामके बिरह सहा नहीं जातहो,
गोरी सोचनमें तन छाय ॥३॥

पियपिय बोल पपिहरा बोलत सुनि सुनि धीर न आये ॥

लालबिहारी धीर धरावत,
गोरी धीर धरो मन माय ॥४॥

Chautal

Sakhi, as soon as I wake, I dress
as spring, with armlets,
bangles, and rings. The necklace
around my throat gleams

like my forehead's bindi.
I sit on the bed and call,
Piya. Piya. Don't tell me any news
of him, don't tell me

I've wasted my life. My blouse
bursts; my whole body aches
for him. This distance between us
I cannot bear. I am lost.

The papiha bird cries, *Piya.*
Piya. Hearing this unstitches me.

Lalbihari: "Peace. Peace."

उलारा

गोरि तेरे नयना कजर भल सोहे,
गोरि तेरे नयना कजर भल सोहे ॥
बांकि चितवनते जग मोहे,
गोरि तेरे नयना कजर भल सोहे ॥

Ulara

Fair one, your eye's kohl
bewitches me.
Your spark ensnares
the world; the kajar
of your eyes
possesses.

चौताल

अब लिखन चहत कुछु गांव सुनो चित धारी ॥
गांवहै गुड्डुहुप अरु पीनजारी गुडीनटेन्ट अतिभारी ॥

अतिरमणीक सुथल थल रोराहो,
तहां रामप्रसादके जारी ॥ १ ॥

रामनरायण करहै बोनी फेर फील पीटफोरी ॥

शिवपुर सब बाकीठकहं जानत,
आगेकी रीक बहे सुचि बारी ॥ २ ॥

ता आगे एरी हाल लिखतहौं अलबेंचा धनसारी ॥

बरनन करों आना नीमीपुरकेहो,
तहां सोद्दीहै थानेदारी ॥ ३ ॥

राजमरैया नगर कहावत तहं हमार जिमीदारी ॥

गोलपीलीस सुरधाम सो राजत,
तहां बसतहैं लालबीहारी ॥ ४ ॥

Chautal

Now I write about my village,
listen closely. In the villages Good Hope
and Good Intent aru and pin
are plenty. The earth is good where

Ramprasad dwells. Ramnarayan
sews, and Fairfield is a wetland.
In Shivpur, everyone knows
what lines flow from speech.

I write of the conditions
to come in the tune Raga Dhanasari.
To tell the story, come to Nimipur
where everyone bargains. Telling

Rajmaraiya town's folklore
is my burden; Golden Fleece is the silver-
haven, where Lalbihari dwells.

चौताल

पीयवा परदेसमें छाये सन्देस न आये ॥
सुन्दर मास फगुनवा सजनी पियबिन मोहिं न भाये ॥

पियपिय बोल पपिहरा बोलत,
सुनि कामबिरह तनु छाये ॥१॥

बारे सैयां परदेस निकलगये नहिं कुछ खबर जनाये ॥

नाग वो बाण बरस अब गुजरेहो,
मन अधिक उठत घबड़ाये ॥२॥

छाड़ि जनाना घर मरदाना पीयकर खोज कराये ॥

धीर धरों जिय धीर न आवत,
तहं योबन जोर जनाये ॥३॥

निसिदिन बैठि पिया दिस देखत अबहुं पिया नहीं आये ॥

लालबिहारी बिरह बस कामिनि,
पिय आइके बिरह छोरड़ाये ॥४॥

Chautal

From abroad Piya sends
no word. I'm listless in the month
of Phagun without my love.
The papiha bird cries out, *piya*—

I'm overcome by this distance between us.
He stole away to another country
without telling me. The rain falls
like arrows or serpents, stirring worry

in my heart. All of the men
of my house go to search for him.
How can I be patient when my youth
itself is a poisoned arrow? Night and day

I sit watching for any sign.
My love has not yet returned.

Lalbihari
is just a resonance chamber, the beloved
will come and banish your pain.

चौताल

पिया कैसे चले मदमाते रैन कहँ सोय ॥
नई नारी घर तेहिसंग राजे ताहीसे अलसाय ॥

चाल चलत हाथीजस झूमत,
मानो रंगभरे तनु आय ॥१॥

सात पांच कर ऐ सखी आय लिया देखि हर्षाय ॥

नवसत तासु लियाकर साजति,
एतो देखि नयन मुसकाय ॥२॥

सांच कहो हमसे तुम बालम काहेके सरमाय ॥

पकड़ि गये अब बोलत नाहीहो,
मानो हमसे तो अधिक डेराय ॥३॥

एतनी बात सुने सखियनसे मनहीमन घबड़ाय ॥

लालबिहारी कहें सुनु सखियाहो,
मैंतो गंग नहानेके जाय ॥४॥

Chautal

Did he sway and walk, drunk
at night? Where did he sleep?
He's probably living with another
woman who makes him lazy.

His gait is like an elephant painted
purple. Having done his seventy-five
good works, he delights in women.
I imagine he sees her eyes

and smiles. Why are you ashamed,
tell me truly? Being caught
you say nothing, as though you fear me.
Hearing this, may the listener

become restless. Lalbihari says,
"I am going to bathe in the Ganga River."

उलारा

पिया ना आया परदेसी,
मोर पिया ना आया परदेसी ॥
होली फाग मचावत गावत,
मोर जिया हो मोर जिया
ललचाय सखीरी ॥
पिया ना आया परदेसी ॥

Ulara

Spring songs
sound.

My heart
craves you,
my friend,
who has not yet
returned.

चौताल

सखि आयो बसंत बहार पिया नहिं आये ॥
फागुन मस्त महीना सखिया मोर जिया ललचाये ॥

सब नर नारी जो फागुन गावत,
सखि मोकहं सूल बढ़ाये ॥१॥

ताल मृदंग झांझ डफ बाजे सबको मन हरषाये ॥

मैं बिरहिनि सेजियापर बिलखति,
मोहिं अजु मदन तनु छाये ॥२॥

भरभरके पिचकारी मारत नात गोत बिलगाये ॥

सखि सब घर घर धूम मचावत,
तहां रंग अबिरन छाये ॥३॥

गारी देत सभीको सबही ना कोइ काहु लजाये ॥

लालबिहारी विरहबस बनिताहो,
सोतो बैठे मनहि सुझाये ॥४॥

Chautal

Sakhi, spring has come, yet
my beloved has not. In Phagun
my heart yearns. All who sing
Phagun, all drums that beat

light rhythms, twist the dagger
in my heart. In longing I sob
into my bed, drunk
with this sickness.

Pichkaris filled with color,
every house raises celebration.
Raining down on all,
colorful streams.

Abuse goes all around,
today no one's shy.

                Lalbihari says,
"The one who suffers separation
sits alone, heart wilting."

चौताल

सखि आया बसंत बहार चलो ब्रिज ओरी ॥
सब सखियनके झुण्ड भयेहैं हाथ कनक पिचकारी ॥

तकितकि मारत स्यामके मुखपर,
तहां कृष्ण हँसत दै तारी ॥ १ ॥

राधे सैन कियो सखियनके कृष्ण लियो सब घेरी ॥

फाग खेलावत कृष्णके सखि सब,
तहां सब्द उठत घनघोरी ॥ २ ॥

बाजत ताल मृदंग झांझ डफ जैजैकार पुकारी ॥

बृन्दाबनके कुंज गलिनमें हो,
तहां फाग मची अतिभारी ॥ ३ ॥

खेलत फाग परसपर हिलिमिलि सोभित तहं बनवारी ॥

लालबिहारी कृष्णगुण गावत,
तहां फाग रचे चितधारी ॥ ४ ॥

Chautal

Sakhi, spring has come,
let's go to Brij.
All friends clutch pichkaris
and spray Shyam's face,

Krishna laughs and claps.
Radha's confidantes circle Krishna
as an army. Krishna, Radha,
and all of her companions

play Holi, the air thick.
Drums beat out joy
as the people cry out.
Vrindavan's wooded glens swell,

heavy with Holi. Each player
remarks on Banvari's beauty.

Lalbihari sings of Krishna's goodness
and writes Phaag devotedly.

उलारा

चलु देखि आइ भोलाके कुंजगलिया,
चलु केखि आइ भोलाके कुंजगलिया ॥
कौने लगाया बेला चमेला,
कौने लगाया बेला चमेला ॥
कौने लगाया अनार कलिया,
चलु देखि आइ भोलाके कुंजगलिया ॥
गौरा लगाया बेला चमेला,
गौरा लगाया बेला चमेला ॥
भोला लगाया अनार कलिया,
चलु देखि आइ भोलाके कुंजगलिया ॥

Ulara

Let's go and see Bhola's forested lanes,
its gardens and vales.
Who there planted the jasmines?
Let's go see.

Gaura planted the jasmine and Bhola
the pomegranate buds.

चौताल

सखियै सन प्रीति लगावै पिया मन भावै ॥
जस नटिनी चढ़िजात बांसपर गहिके ढोल बजावै ॥

खेल देखावत लोग रिझावत,
वहतौ सुरत बांसपर लावै ॥१॥

जैसे पतंग जरे दीपकमें तन मन फूँकि जरावै ॥

ओइसे पतिव्रत जरत पियासंग,
वहतौ सकल सोच बिसरावै ॥२॥

जैसे पपिहरा पियरट लावे पियादरस नहिं पावै ॥

वह पंछी अंडाकहं सेवत,
वहतौ पलभरि नहिं बिसरावै ॥३॥

साधु यती सुर असुर समरमें इनको कवन बचावै ॥

लालबिहारी कहत संतनसेहो,
सखि ऐसी रहनि लखि पावै ॥४॥

Chautal

Sakhi, I love him so. I am
an aerialist ascending
a pole, my heart thrumming
like a dhol drum. I awe

the crowd with twists.
Like a moth burning up,
my body and mind are flame.
With my beloved beside me,

I forget the world. A papiha
cries out *piya* and never sees
her beloved, she never forgets
to care for her clutch of eggs.

A sadhu saves both gods and demons
on the battlefield, who will save him?

Lalbihari says, "Saints,
may the lover find such a perch."

चौताल

मोरे गवनके दिन नगिचाने चलब ससुरारी ॥
पहिल पठौनी तिन जन आये नौवा ब्राह्मण बारी ॥

जाइकहो मोरे बारे बलमसेहो,
सैंया अब कि लगन देउ टारी ॥ १ ॥

तनसारी अनुराग लहंगवा प्रेमके डोरि सम्भारी ॥

सुरतिके सेन्दुर मांग सँवारत,
दृग अंजनरेख सवांरी ॥ २ ॥

आयहें चारि कहार बलमसंग द्वारपर डोली उतारी ॥

धै बहियां डोलिया बैठावत,
तहं कोइ न लाग गोहारी ॥ ३ ॥

रोवनलगी संगकी सखियां होनलगी तैयारी ॥

लालबिहारी जग नैहर छूटत,
सखि रामभजन हितकारी ॥ ४ ॥

Chautal

My days are ending, I will go
to my in-law's home. People come
with a boat and a Brahmin.
Go to my beloved and tell him,

"Stop this. Come home."
My body's sari is spun of love's threads.
I've put vermillion in my hair,
streaked kohl on my eyes.

Four men come to lay
a palanquin at my door.
Taking me by the arms,
they seat me on it; everyone

cries out. My friends begin
to weep as they make preparations.

           Lalbihari says,
"Leaving the world of your parent's home
singing praises to Rama will help."

चौताल

उठी जगुनसंत खेलाड़ी नया बैपारी ॥
जबसे तुमतो लादिचलेहो पांच चोर संग भारी ॥

इनसे सजग रहो निसिबासर,
नत लुटिलेत बनिजारी ॥१॥

पांच पचीस संग नित धावत धात लगावत भारी ॥

जब अपनी अवसर करिपावत,
तहं देतहैं काज बिगारी ॥२॥

सोवतहौ तुम खोवत गठरी मालधनीके भारी ॥

करु रघुनाथ भजन तन मनसेहो,
इहां आइहै निसि अंधिअरी ॥३॥

कहे सुने कोइ बात न माने देखे नयन उघारी ॥

लालबिहारी संत सौदागर,
लखि छोड़िदीन नवनारी ॥४॥

Chautal

Saints and brothers wake up!
Your senses will rob you
of your attention.
Guard against them day and

night. They run away with you
and carve great pain
without you even knowing.
Given the chance,

they ruin everything. Sleeping,
you will lose all your wealth.
Sing praises to Raghunath
in this night's darkness.

No one will listen to this who
doesn't believe their eyes—

        Lalbihari says,
"Saint and merchant, don't be seduced."

चौताल

मोसे बरबस फाग मचाई करै चतुराई ॥
सुनि बाजत तहं ढोल मजीरा सोवत कन्त जगाई ॥

फाग खेलनकहं जाब बलम
हम मोरि सखियन बोलि पठाई ॥१॥

लै आग्या प्रीतमकी सुन्दरि सजि सिंगार बनाई ॥

गजगति चलत हलत नकबेसर,
तहं कमलन हार सोहाई ॥२॥

बजी बांसुरी स्यामसुन्दरकी सब सखियन उठिधाई ॥

वंसीके तान बानसम लागत,
मोसे सुनिके रहा नहिं जाई ॥३॥

चलीं मिलन सब नन्दलालसों मनकी तपनबुझाई ॥

लालबिहारीरसके बस मोहन,
सबसखियनके मनभाई ॥४॥

Chautal

Come smear my body with color.
Hearing the dhol and majira,
the sleeping deva wakes.
Beloved, my friends ask, "Where

will we go to play Holi?
With permission,
they bedeck themselves.
With the grace of an elephant's gait,

they sport lotus garlands.
When Krishna's flute calls,
all women leap.
His tune is an arrow—

hearing it, who is not slain?
All rush to him, hearts
set on fire.

Lalbihari says, "Mohan, I'm yours."

चौताल

उठुरी बृषभानकिसोरी मची बृज होरी ॥
चलो सखी बृज देखन चलिये, सासु ननदकी चोरी ॥

ग्वालसखा सब ताल बजावत,
तहं नाचत राधा गोरी ॥ १ ॥

बंसीबट जमुनातट मोहन, इत उत फाग रचोरी ॥

बंसीके सब्द सुनत सब सखियन,
तहं साज सजी एक ठौरी ॥ २ ॥

सावन मास तरुण जस बरषा, रंग उड़ै चहुँ ओरी ॥

चहुंदिसि कीच मची जमुनापर,
तहं अबिर गुलाल भरो री ॥ ३ ॥

लचकि लचकि मन मोहन नाचें, सखी हंसत मुख मोरी ॥

लालबिहारी कहत कर जोरीहो,
दोऊ अमर रहे या जोरी ॥ ४ ॥

Chautal

Wake up! They are playing
Holi in Brij. Let's go there
without telling our mothers-in-law.
The Ahir beats rhythms,

Radha dances. By the river Jamuna,
Krishna plays his flute
while people compose Phaag.
Listening to his lilt,

women freeze. In the month
of Saavan, youth rains.
Everywhere the colors of Holi
fly. All about the Jamuna

is the mud of colors, of abir.
Mohan dances and dances,
dazzles onlookers.

           Lalbihari says,
"May this couple remain for all time."

चौताल

मोहा ढूढ़त भयो भिनुसार मिले नहीं प्यारा ॥
भूख प्यास निद्रा नहीं आवै तलफत प्राण हमारा ॥

मधु रस मुरलीके सब्द सुनत मोहिं,
सब छूटिगये सुख सारा ॥ १ ॥

जंत्र तंत्र औ मंत्र न लागे, औषध मूल हजारा ॥

ब्याकुल पूछत पत्र लतनसेहो,
तुम देखेहु नन्दकुमारा ॥ २ ॥

हे चंपा धरती औ तुलसी तुम हौ मित्र हमारा ॥

हरी हरी करत रहत निसि बासर,
तेरो श्रीपति प्राण हमारा ॥ ३ ॥

अन्तरध्यान भये छनहीमें नन्दजसोमतीबारा ॥

लालबिहारीके सूझ परत नहीं,
मोही कृष्ण लगावहु पारा ॥ ४ ॥

Chautal

I've searched for ages;
my beloved's nowhere. I can't
hunger or thirst. Sleep is a distant dream.
I am in misery. After drinking in

his flute, peace is a myth.
No charm, no magic, no mantra,
no medicine cures my restlessness.
I ask leaves and plants,

"Have you glimpsed Krishna?"
O Jasmine, Earth, and Tulsi,
you are my only friends. Night and day
I cry, *Hari. Hari.*

In a split-second Nanda-Yashomati's
beloved son disappeared
into the forest. Lalbihari is blind
to all else but Krishna, so help.

चौताल

सैंयां दूरी न करौ जवाइ बसंत अवाई ॥
पैयां परौं कर जोरि मनावों, धरि बहियाँ समुझाई ॥

मानो तो मानो पिय अरज हमारीहो,
नाहीं नैहर उमिरि बिताई ॥ १ ॥

बीती रैन अनलके भीतर, बिरह बिथा तनु छाई ॥

पिय पिय करत पिया नहिं देखत,
गोरि तलफके रैनि बिताई ॥ २ ॥

चोलिनके बन्द तड़कनलागे नयन नीर भरिआई ॥

मन पछितात हाथ दो मीजत,
सब सुधि बुधि जात भुलाई ॥ ३ ॥

जब सुधि आवत पिय अपनेके, प्राण बहुत दुखपाई ॥

लालबिहारीके रसबस होगई,
तहं नयनमें नयन मिलाई ॥ ४ ॥

Chautal

Don't go far, it's spring.
I hold your arms and beg.
Piya, I cry, though you remain
my youth in my parent's home.

At night without you,
pain's flames bite me. *Piya*,
piya, I cry, though you remain
invisible. Krishna, I spend

my nights so. The hooks
of my blouse cut into my skin,
tears well in my eyes.
The heart regrets, and wringing

my two hands I'm a fool.
It will be painful when my senses return.
Labihari's dance has finished.
Come, let our eyes meet.

चौताल

मोसे घरमें रहा नहिं जात समलियाहो प्यारे ॥
कीतौ मोहन मोर संग लगौ कीघररहो हमारे ॥

अबतौ लाज छूटि सब तनकेहो,
तुमहौ पति प्राण हमारे ॥ १ ॥

अबतौ प्रीति लगिगई तुमसे सुनौ जसोमतिबारे ॥

नयन हमार तुमै बिन देखत,
नहिं मानत सांझ सकारे ॥ २ ॥

घरके लोग भये सब बैरी, मात पिता सब हारे ॥

प्रीति लगी कबहुँ नहिं छूटत,
मोरे नयन भये रतनारे ॥ ३ ॥

सुनि बानी बृषभानसुताकी बिहँसे नन्ददुलारे ॥

लालबिहारी कमल मुख निरखत,
मोहि बिसरत नाहिं बिसारे ॥ ४ ॥

Chautal

I can't stay inside, take me
with you, Mohan. Love, tell me,
"Come with me." I'm shameless
for you, my life. Now love

finds you. Listen, son of Yashomati.
Without you I can't tell
dawn from dusk, family from foe,
mother from father. I've lost everything.

Love once faceted does not abate;
my eyes have become jewels.

Hearing Radha's voice,
Nanda's beloved son laughs.

           Lalbihari says,
"The lotus face can't be forgotten,
no matter how you try."

चौताल

कैसे बीते गवनवांके राति घटा लगी कारी ॥
कबहुँ न सोवत पिय तुमरे संग तलफि तलफि जिय जारी ॥

बारे बलम मोरी सेज न आवत,
सैयां मारत बिरह कटारी ॥१॥

सारि उमिरिया नैहर बीती, जानेउ दरद न मोरी ॥

नाहक ब्याह कियो पिया हमसेहो,
बरु नैहर रहतिउं कुवांरी ॥२॥

गोली लगे हिया बिच सहिये सहिये मन तरवारी ॥

पियके बोल हियाबिच सालत,
मोरे मनमें करत दुखारी ॥३॥

कबहुँ न कीन्ह पियासंग बातैं, न भरि नयन निहारी ॥

लालबिहारी पछितात मनहि मन,
मैं तो केहिसे कहों दुख भारी ॥४॥

Chautal

Dark clouds gather at night.
Piya leaves my bed;
my life hisses as it burns.
My beloved does not come

even though I litter my sheets
with flowers. He stabs me
with the frozen dagger
of distance. I squander my youth

in my father's home, no one
knows my pain. I may as well
remain a virgin or have a bullet
or sword pierce my heart.

Tell my beloved my chest pains me.
Since my love and I don't speak,
he has not seen my tears.

              Lalbihari regrets,
"Who do I tell of this heartbreak?"

चौताल

तुम सुनहु जसोमति माई स्याम दधि खाई ॥
सखा संगलिये मोहि खिझावत माखन देत लुटाई ॥

माखन खात मही ढरकावत,
मोरी गेरु लि लेत चोराई ॥ १ ॥

मैंतो चलीजात मारगमें बरबस मोहि बिलमाई ॥

माखन चाखनके हित कारन,
बिन कामसे रारि मचाई ॥ २ ॥

पकरि पकरिके चोली खोलत लाजकी बात सुनाई ॥

ऐसे निलज्ज भये मनमोहन,
धरि अंचल संग लपटाई ॥ ३ ॥

देखत छोट खोट बातनमें, मोहिसे कहा न जाई ॥

लालबिहारी कमलमुख निरखत,
हंसि बोलत बात बनाई ॥ ४ ॥

Chautal

Listen, mother Yashomati,
Shyam ate all the malai.
He and his friends annoy me
by stealing all the butter.

Eating the yogurt spilled
on the floor, he steals my clothes.
On the road, he stops me,
snacking on curd,

complaining. He catches me
and undoes my blouse,
speaking to me. So shameless
is Mohan, he burns

my skirt, my breast. Look,
he does so many things
listing them all is impossible.

                Lalbihari says,
"Laughing, he makes his point."

चौताल

ऋतु आये बसन्त बहार कन्त मुख मोरी ॥
लैके अबिर गुलाल अरगजा केसरमें सरबोरी ॥

चोली चीर चुन्दरिया अपनीहो,
पियवा लेइके रंग घोरी ॥ १ ॥

सब सखि सोवत अपने महलमें पीया गले कर जोरी ॥

बिरहबिथा सहिजात न मोहिसन,
उठि ताकत मथुराकी खोरी ॥ २ ॥

गेंद रसाल फुले बन टेसू भँवर कली बैठो री ॥

दादुर मोर पपिहरा बोलत,
सखि कैसेके धीर धरो री ॥ ३ ॥

ऊधो जाइ कहो माधोसे, कवन चूक भई मोरी ॥

नन्दलला कुबरी बस होइगये,
हंसि कहतहैं लालबिहारी ॥ ४ ॥

Chautal

The spring blooms
upon my face. Mix the abir
with saffron. My love tears
my blouse and veil

as he brazenly colors me.
While my companions sleep,
my beloved compels me. I can't bear
separation. Weak, I rise

and stare towards Mathura.
On the marigold blooms
a black bee perches, while frogs,
papiha, and peacocks sing. Sakhi,

how to keep my peace? As Krishna,
what sin have I committed?

"Has Nandalal's beloved become
a hunchbacked maid?" laughs Lalbihari.

Bhajan
भजन

पहिला भजन

प्रभुजी तुम बिन कवन सहाइ ॥
सब अपने अपने स्वारथके, कुटुम लोग अरु भाइ ॥ १ ॥
संपतसे मिलाई राखत, गुण अवगुण न गनाइ ॥
बिपतिपरे कोइ संग न लागत, छाँड़त मीत मीताइ ॥ २ ॥
घर नारी गारी बहु भाखत, नित उठि करत लड़ाइ ॥
साधुजननमें दोष लगावत, निन्दा करत पराइ ॥ ३ ॥
सबबिधि दीन जानि जन अपनो, कृपा करो रघुराइ ॥
सिन्धु अथाह बहो मैं जाता, तुम बिन कवन सहाइ ॥ ४ ॥
ज्यों गज औ प्रहलाद उबारे महिमा ध्रुवहि देखाइ ॥
विपति बिदारण पतित उधारण, तुमरो गुन बहुताइ ॥ ५ ॥
कीजे लाज नाम अपनेकी, मोर संकट मेटो आइ ॥
लालबिहारी दीन पुकारत, राखिलेहु सरनाइ ॥ ६ ॥

First Bhajan

Prabhu, who else but you
buttresses me? Everyone
is out for themselves only,
family and brothers
keeping friends for wealth,
not because they are special.
In times of turmoil, every friend
deserts me. In the house
my wife insults me,
wages war as soon as dawn.
She even finds flaws in sadhus.
I'm a wretch needing mercy,
Rama. As the Sindhu river
flows unfathomed, I, too, go.
Who else but you is my rescue?
How you saved Gaj, Prahlad,
and, through Dhruv, your majesty shone.
You reveal your power
and uplift the abject, the ill,
the miserable. Your virtues
are measureless. Keeping
with your repute, come;
erase my peril.
The wretched Lalbihari pleads,
"Shelter me."

दूसरा भजन

जो नर निसिदिन रामनाम गुण गावत निस्सन्देह
आनन्दसहित सो, भक्ति मुक्ति फल पावत ॥ १ ॥
काल ब्याल दूरते कांपत, यम नेरे नहिं आवत ॥
सेवा करत पार्षद निसिदिन, ठाढे चंवर ढुरावत ॥ २ ॥
सुन्दर सुभग बिमान सजाकर, सब मिल ताहि चढावत ॥
संख मृदंग बजाय धूमसे, परमधाम पहुंचावत ॥ ३ ॥
राम राम कहि जात रामपुर, रामदास कहलावत ॥
लालबिहारी भक्तिकी महिमा, सेस पार नहीं पावत ॥ ४ ॥

Second Bhajan

For bliss, for liberation,
sing Rama's name daily.
Time trembles from afar,
the Lord of Death
will not come near.
Night and day your servants
and councilors will gently
fan you. Adorning your vehicle
they will scramble to seat you.
Playing conch and knocking
the mridang drum with joy,
they will lead you
to the highest abode.
Chanting *Rama Rama*
they will take you to Rampur
and call you Ramdas,
servant of Rama. Lalbihari says,
"Who can find the limits
of such faith?"

तीसरा भजन

सन्तोंकी महिमा अपरम्पार ॥
सत्संगति सम धर्म न दूजा, कहरहे बेद पुकार ॥ १ ॥
जप, तप, नियम, ध्यान, व्रत, संयम, कीजे बर्ष हजार ॥
कठिनाईसे मिलत परमपद, कोटिनबिन्घ विकार ॥ २ ॥
सत्संगतसे तुरत होत नर, भवसागरसे पार ॥
संगतिकी महिमा सेस संभु अज, जानत भलीप्रकार ॥ ३ ॥

Third Bhajan

The greatness of the saints
is unmatched. All of the Vedas cry out:

there is no path greater
than keeping good company.

Mastery of chanting,
of mantras, austerities, control,

fasting, meditation:
all take one thousand years.

Only with difficulty
do you reach the highest place,

thwarting one million obstacles.
Yet in the company of great ones,

you can cross the seas
of illusion in an instant.

Now, the benefits of this
Shambu well knows.

With the help of this satsang,
the sages Vashishta and Narad attain

consciousness. With Luv
and Nimesh, it doesn't take four eons.

सत्संगतिसे वसिष्ठ अरु नारद, कीन्हो ब्रह्मविचार॥
लव निमेषके संगति करिके लग न सकत युग चार॥४॥
सत्संगतिकी महिमा ऐसी, जो धरी सेस महिभार॥
लालबिहारी कहाँ लगि बरने, सन्तन मोहि उधार॥५॥

The power of satsang is like this,
it carries the weight of eternity.

Lalbihari alone can't describe it:
"Help me, O saints."

चौथा भजन

यह मन मायामें लपटानो ॥
कथा रामकी झूठ सब जगत, घंटा संख बजानो ॥ १ ॥
बारबार समझावतहूं मैं, क्यौं तुम भयो दिवानो ॥
झूठे घरको सत्य बतावत, सांचो गेह भुलानो ॥ २ ॥
अबहुँ समुझ नाहिं कुछ बिगडो ज्यौंका त्यौं सब जानो ॥
जब यह प्राण छुटिजायंगे, तब करिहें पछितानो ॥ ३ ॥
चौरासीमें तब भटकत फिरीहें, कहुँ नहिं लगे ठेकानो ॥
अन्तसमय कोई संग न साथी, यमपुर है तब जानो ॥ ४ ॥

Fourth Bhajan

Illusion's fire lights the mind.
Believing Rama mere myth,

they ring the bells
and blow the conch.

I try and try to make you see
you are going mad. You forget

the true house and call it false.
Now you can't tell the ruined

from the real, the true
from the imitation.

When this life draws to a close,
you will have such regret,

you will wander the eighty-four lakhs
of births and deaths

without peace or rest.
At the end of time

you will enter Yampur,
the City of the Dead, alone.

Lalbihari is of no use;
you are alone and destitute.

लालबिहारी काम नहिं आवत, अपनो अवर बिरानो ॥
सब संसार स्वपनकी माया, सच्चा रामनाम गुण गानो ॥५॥

This whole creation is a dream-
like illusion. Sing the only truth

of Rama's name.

पांचवां भजन

बिन हरिभजन कवन सुखपायो ॥
रामके नाम परस सुखदायक, सब सन्तन मिलिगायो ॥ १ ॥
जिन सब झूँठ प्रपंच मोह तजि रामसों नेह लगायो ॥
निःसन्देह यह देह त्यागकर रामसमीप बसायो ॥ २ ॥
सबभक्तनमेंभक्त सिरोमणि, पूरणभक्त कहायो ॥
करत पुराणप्रशंसा निसिदिन, त्रिभुवनमें जस छायो ॥ ३ ॥
भक्तहेत भगवान जगतमें, मनुष रूप धरि आयो ॥
दुष्ट मारि भूभार उतारत, आनन्द सबन देखायो ॥ ४ ॥
भक्तिभावसे सेस सीसपर भूको भार उठायो ॥
लालबिहारी रहत सरननमे, रामचरण मन भायो ॥ ५ ॥

Fifth Bhajan

Without singing praises to Hari,
who will attain bliss?
Rama's name is the joy
all the saints sing about.
All who, for Rama, sacrifice the lies
that yoke them to the world
will dwell with him
when they slough off
their bodies; of all the devout,
he is the greatest.
Singing the Puranas, his fame spreads
throughout all three worlds.
On behalf of the devotee, the Lord
took human form and came to earth
and slew the evil, bestowing
joy to all. Feeling for the devout,
he lessened the burdens
carried in their heads.
Lalbihari remains in the refuge
at Rama's feet.

छठवां भजन

भजो भाई हरिहर हरिहर हरिहर ॥
आदिब्रह्मअद्वैत निरंजन, भयभंजन धरणीधर ॥ १ ॥
जब भक्तनको असुर सतावत, प्रगट होत तेहि अवसर ॥
दुष्ट मारि भुभार उतारत, बिश्वनाथ बिश्वंभर ॥ २ ॥
कबहुं बिहार करत भक्तनसंग, धरि धरिरूप मनोहर ॥
कबहुँ संहार करत सब जगके, धरकर भेष भयंकर ॥ ३ ॥
ऐसे प्रभुको भजन करो तुम, मनलगाय निसिबासर ॥
लालबिहारी कहत सबहीसे, भजु मन रामचरण शिव शंकर ॥ ४ ॥

Sixth Bhajan

Sing brothers,
    Harihar.
        Harihar.
            Harihar.

The initial greatness is whole,
unblemished, and removes fear.
The moment demons molest

the devout, he appears,
destroys all evil, takes away
the pains of the world.

This is the lord of the world, Lord Shiva.
With his devotees he wanders
in beautiful form. Sometimes

he destroys creation,
taking incarnation. Sing
of such a Lord night and day.

To all, Lalbihari says,
"Sing *Shiv-Shankar* at Rama's feet."

सातवां भजन

प्रभुकी महिमा अपरम्पार ॥
पढत बिरंचि बेद नित चारो, तेहु न पावत पार ॥ १ ॥
सेस महेस गणेस अरु सारद, निसि दिन करत बिचार ॥
हारमान चुप रहत रटत फिर, उरमें धीरज धार ॥ २ ॥
बाल्मीकि नारद बसिष्ठ भृगु, खोजत बारम्बार ॥
नेति नेति कर कहत परसपर, धन्य धन्य करतार ॥ ३ ॥
बड़े बड़े सिद्ध सकल योगीजन, तन मन धन सब वार ॥
लालबिहारी लेत सरणागत, समुझत जगत अधार ॥ ४ ॥

Seventh Bhajan

Prabhu's greatness is incalculable.
Those who make it through
all the Vedas don't get it.
Shesh, Mahesh, Ganesh, and Sarad
meditate on it unceasingly.
Accepting defeat, they stuff
their chests with silence.
Patience is the blade
Valmiki, Narad, Vashishta,
and Bhrigu search and search for.
"Not this. Not this," they say to
one another. "Bless Khartar."
The great, the accomplished,
yogis hold him in their minds and hearts.
Lalbihari takes refuge and knows
the foundation of this world.

आठवां भजन

रबिहीं सकल बस्तु उपजावै ॥
भांति भांतिके फल पुष्पादिक, सुभ सुगंध महकावै ॥ १ ॥
जो जो बस्तु रची ब्रह्माने, सबमें झलक देखावै ॥
सबमें तेज सूर्जका भासे, पाले और सुखावै ॥ २ ॥
आठ मासमें जो जल सोखत, चार मास बरसावै ॥
ओही जलसे अन्न अनेकन, बृक्ष लता प्रगटावे ॥ ३ ॥
जेठ माससे तपत दसो दिस, अग्निरूप दरसावै ॥
लालबिहारी इष्ट कर मानत, पूरण ब्रह्म करावै ॥ ४ ॥

Eighth Bhajan

Only from god
do all things come.

Fruits and flowers,
their intoxicating perfumes,

in every single thing
you can see Brahma:

in the blazing sun, energy
and heat. The same water

that dries up for eight months
rains down for four months.

From this cycle
he makes many grains,

trees, and vines grow.
In the month of Jeth,

in the heat from ten directions,
he shows himself.

Lalbihari's ishta deva,
his beloved deity,

is called the whole Brahma.

कावित्त

जाके सुद्ध हिया ताके आनुभव होत
तुव नाथ निज तेजहीसे माया गुणनासीहै॥
जगतके ब्यापी निज जापीको अतापी करै,
नाम रूप आपके अनन्त दिब्य भासीहै॥
आपके समान नहिं अधिक कहाँते होय
अहंकार क्षार होत ध्यान मुदरासी है॥
कालत्रास नास तत्काल करि सुख देत,
डमरानिवासी कहै लालजुविहारीहै॥
नरअवतार नहीं केवल दनुजकुल
नासनके हेतु यह परन विचारीहै॥
जनन सिखाइबेको औरहुं देखाइबेको
नारिके अधीन जैसे होत दुख भारीहै॥
अवधनिवासी सीतासंगके विलासी,
जगतकेर हौ प्रकासी कौन उचित खंभारी है॥
तजिके निबेस जाय कानन कलेस सहे,
धन्य सो धरामें अवधेसके कुमार है॥
कहत सोच लालबिहारी सुनो भाई कान देइ,
ओही राम सत्य करके सत्य सत्य इष्ट हैं॥

Kavitt

Whoever has a clear heart
    will feel you, Lord,
despite this dazzling web
    of illusion. In the world,
those who sing their own
    self-praises suffer.
Your names and forms
    are countless and majestic.
No one is like you;
    even pride is rendered useless.
Meditation is like a mudra.
    "Destroying all the world's evil
in an instant, you give peace,"
    says Lalbihari, who lives in Demerara.

Not only to destroy countless demons
    did he take human form,
but also to show
    how being in a woman's thrall
brings misery. Dwelling in Awadh,
    the one who will shine light and make right,
who desires Sita's company,
    is worth contemplating.
Leaving home to endure
    the hardships of the forest,
auspiciousness is placed
    on the Prince of Awadh.
Lalbihari thinks and says,
    "Listen, brothers, give me your ears:
you make Rama into truth
    when truth itself is truth."

सवैया

बुद्धि बड़ी चतुराइ बड़ी मनमें ममता अतिही लपटीहै ॥
नाम बड़ी धनवान बडी करतूति बडी जगमें प्रगटी है ॥
गज बाजि ही द्वार मनुष्य हजार तौ इन्द्र समानसे कौन घटी है ॥
सो सब रामके भक्ति विना मनो सुन्दर नारिकी नाक कटीहै ॥
ऐसो विचार भजो श्रीरामहीं मोह प्रपंचको त्याग झठीहै ॥
लालबिहारीकहें समुझाइ संगत साधुके नित्यसचीहै ॥

Savaiya

No matter how intelligent you are,
whatever is dear to your heart
will burn in flames. However renowned
your name, however rich, whatever
great deeds you have revealed in this world,
one thousand elephants and people
at your door are less than Indra
fleeing in great fear. Those
without faith in Rama
are like a beautiful woman
with her nose hacked
off. Sing these thoughts of Rama,
give up your attachments
and desires.

  Lalbihari says, "Try and understand,
the company of saints is absolute truth."

दोहा

भई कृपा जब मोहिंपर, पूरणभइयह गाथ॥
करहु कृपा मोहिं जानि जन, तुम प्रभु दीनानाथ॥१॥

लालबिहारी नाम है, रहै डमराके बीच॥
कामकरे सरकारके, संग करे नहिं नीच॥२॥ इति

इति लालबिहारीकृत डमराफागबहार समाप्त।

Doha

I am blessed that I have completed my tale.
O Lord of the wretched, show mercy.

My name is Lalbihari, I live in Demerara,
I work for the crown and stay far from the wicked.

Here ends Lalbihari Sharma's *Holi Songs of Demerara*.

रामसमुझमहाराज.
बच्चू महाराज.
चुन्नीमहाराज.
शिवबरन महाराज.
सीतल.
बालेसिंह.
बेनीमाधोसिंह.
रघुनन्दसिंह.
पूरन.
त्रिभुवनसिंह.
देवनारायण.
सेसनारायण.
बौधनारायण.
नारायणसिंह.
परमलाल.
लालाराम.
सामलिया.
बिलाससिंह.
शिवबरनसिंह.
चुन्नीमहाराज.
रघुनन्दसिंह.
बिसुनदयाल.
बच्चूमहाराज.
सेसनारायण.
छठुतानी.
रसुलतानी.
कीसुन.

रूपचन्दसिंह.
त्रिभुवनसिंह.
लालाराम.
सीतल.
देवनारायण.
बेनीमाधोसिंह.
सुकदेव.
पंडित परमानन्दजी.
बिसुनदयाल.
राधाकीसुन.
चुन्नीमहाराज.
केवलसिंह.
देवीलाल.
शिवबरनमहाराज.
नारायाणमहाराज.
सामलिया.
छठुतानी.
पूरन.
लालराम.
राधाकिसुन.
देवीलाल.
बौधनारायण.
रसुलतानी.
बच्चूमहाराज.
ब्रह्मनारायण.
सीतल.
सामलिया.

बिक्रमसिंह साधु.
रघुनन्दसिंह.
परमलाल.
पूरन.
विसुनदयाल.
किसुन.
लालाराम.
बौधनरायण.
केवलसिंह.
विसनुदयाल.
शिवबरनमहाराज.
रसुलतानी.
बालेसिंह.
राधाकिसुन.
पूरन.
बिलाससिंह.

१ रामसमुझमहाराज.
२ रूपचन्दसिंह.
३ सेसनरायण.
४ पंडित परमानन्दजी.
५ नारायणसिंह.
६ सुकदेव.
७ बेनीमाधोसिंह.
८ बिक्रमसिंहसाधु.
९ परमलाल.
१० किसुन.
११ बच्चूमहाराज.

१२ देवीलाल.
१३ सीतल.
१४ सामलिया.
१५ चुन्नीमहाराज.
१६ सची.
रघुनन्दसिंह.
त्रिभुवनसिंह.
सची.
ब्रह्मनारायण.
छठुतानी.
लालराम.

१७ बालेसिंह.
१८ बिलाससिंह.
१९ त्रिभुवनसिंह.
२० केवलसिंह.
२१ देवनारायण.
२२ छठुतानी.
२३ शिवबरनमहाराज.
२४ ब्रह्मनारायण.
२५ बौधनारायण.
२६ रसुलतानी.
२७ रघुनन्दसिंह.
२८ राधाकिसुन.
२९ पूरन.
३० विसुनदयाल.
३१ लालाराम.

Transliteration for
Chautal Singers
The Tale of Demerara

chhand

bhumi janam ka prant chhapara ġaanv mairitand hai

brahmadev kar putra jano
lalbihari naam hai

aayke ham baas kinhan
desh damaralok hai

rahat ham hain sharan prabhu ke
katat din sab nik hai

•　•　•

In Chhapra 'e get one village name Mairitaand
an' Brahm-bhagwaan get one pickni

'e name Lalbihari. 'E been come yah-so.
Me de a Demerara an' stay corner gad.

doha

britis guyana desh mein, yadyapi praant anek
kahun vicitra kahu(n) atidukhi, yahnij man kar tek

essequibo prant mei(n), golden fleece ek gaanv hai
ati sundar asthan yeh, sab janat yeh thaanv

pandit paramanand ji, basi jaha(n) kar aahi
sabhi ko voh bidit hai, desh videshan mahi(n)

ramcharan puni bandi kar, mahisur pad man dhaar
pandit ji ke charan yug, hamre praan adhaar

•   •   •

Guyana get plenty place—
good kine an' bad kine

wha' you look fa a-you go fine 'em. All bady
does know Golden Fleece in Essiquibo

a whe' Pandit Paramanand stay.
Dem know fum yah-so til a India.

Me bow in front Ram
he meh praan ke adhar.

chaupai

likhan chaho(n) kuchh damara riti,
sunihai sajjan kari priti
yeh hai desh kudesh apara,
rahat na dharam vivek vichara

desh chaa(n)ri kr damara aai,
aapan nam so kuli likhai
bhajan chaa(n)ri chaa(n)re nij-dharmaa,
chaa(n)ri vedpath karhin kukarmaa

nityakaram jo damara mahi(n),
so ab likho(n) kabitt ke mahi(n)

• • •

Me wan' write little 'bout
    how Demerara deh. Hear,
dis country get bad kine people,
    none bady na get sense.

Me lef' India an' come Demerara side
    an' deh call me "Coolie."
All de ting me been lef' the Bedas
    and so come me shame.

Me wan' write little 'bout how me live
    dis side, so me write dis.

kavitt

baji ghanti panch ki ki handi dini hai charhai
bhat liya hai banai dahi chini milike

kahike anand bhaye dvare aaye sardaar
thadhe karat pukaar aagya de(n) samhaar ke

ab dhoyke saspaan bhaat let hai(n) bharai
chilam tayaar kari dharat samhaar ke

jama bhaye nar naari kaandhe dhare hai(n) kudaari
bhir bhai bhaari pahunche damarhu jaaike

• • •

De bell ring a five a'clack an' de karahi pan de fiyah
     rice and dahi bail wid sugah.
Me eat belly full an' de sardar come a me door,
     fe tell abbi wha' abbi mus' do. Me wash
de karahi an' keep de chowr, an' make de pipe
     fe smoke lil bit. All bady come one time
wid cutlass an' ting, de road na get space
     'e choke up wid mattie.

damara haal

pahile pani mein helay latta kapara ki
bhijai aaye hai(n) sardaar kaam det hai bataai ke

•　•　•

Fus' abbi mus' crass de wata
an' abbi close ovah wet.

De sardar come
fe tell abbi wha' abbi mus' do.

doha

ta paachhe saaheb chala, topi unch lagayai
chabuk linho haath mein, sarpat phuncha aai

•　•　•

Den de sahib come fum behin' mattie
an' wear one hat.

'E tek 'e whip and grabble 'e hass
and come run cornah abbi.

kavitt

buk liyohai nikaal pahuncha kuliyo(n) mein jaai
kam likhat banaai sab dekh dekh ke

jaakar hai kaam khoto taakar paisa linho kaati
karat kharaab meri kayua kampe dekhi ke

damara tapu barjor pulis thana chahu or
ram kahan (n) layeho gariban bhulaike

• • •

'E bring one book come and reach abbi
    an' look abbi wuk done and write 'em doung.
If one abbi na wuk done, 'e vex bad bad
    an' na gi' abbi abbi paisa. When me see dis
me shake bad. Demerara get police
    all about. O gad, dey tek abbi yah-so
and fahget abbi because abbi been poor.

doha

aayi sanichar rangla, khusi nar naari
ordhe panchrang chunari, chali manja drbaari

• • •

Come Sati-day, man an' ooman
all ovah jai.

De ooman wear deh orhni
wha' get plenty colah

an' go corner de managah.

kavitt

koi pahir bajuband koi khadi hai dukandh
kaajar manohar nayano(n) se lagaai ke

aaye sardaar kari kaaj sab ke samhaar
payasa det nar naari saban devaai ke

• • •

De put an all deh bangle dem
    an' stan' wid kajar
in deh eye. De sardar come
    fe gi' abbi paisa
an' 'e gi' abbi all abbi money.

chaupai

bite paanch baris yahi bhanti
chinta sok karat dinaraati

tikat paai man bhayau anandaa

jimi chakorsisu nirakhat chandaa
bhayau pramod dharahi naahi(n) dhiraa

koi sadhu bane fakira

hoi adhir chahu(m) disi dhaavhi(n)
eko jukti na man mein laavhi(n)

• • •

Jus' so abbi dis punish
bad five year. Wid a ticket
me heart cry out
like one burd.

Abbi dis ovah happy, some deh like sadhu
an' some deh like fakir
dance all about. Dem na sabi
wha' go come nex'.

doha

sau mein ek dhiraj dhari, rahe gaanv ke mahi(n)
baat sune sardaatke, khusi rahe manmaahi(n)

•　•　•

'E get only couple
mattie wha' patient.

If dey mine de sardar
deh go stay happy.

Rescued From the Footnotes of History

Afterword · *Gaiutra Bahadur*

My name rings no bell ...
but footnotes know me well
footnotes where history
shows its true colors
and passing reference is flesh

The poet John Agard penned these lines about John Edmonstone, an enslaved man born in British Guiana whose name and influence have been erased in history. Edmonstone is the person who taught Charles Darwin the taxidermy skills he deployed during his famous voyage on the H.M.S. Beagle. His descriptions of the rainforests in his South American native country may have inspired Darwin to explore the tropics. Yet Edmonstone, muse and teacher, was not acknowledged.

In Agard's poem, "The Ascent of John Edmonstone," footnotes are where history shows its true colors: they reveal how power held or withheld have muted the contributions of people like Edmonstone. To be called a footnote to history is usually a pejorative, a put-down. I would, however, like to rehabilitate existence in a footnote here. To have been footnoted is to have been cited. To have been cited is to have been published. Lalbihari Sharma, author of the songbook you hold in your hands, also could have declared: *Footnotes know me*. And that, in the archives of indenture, is an accomplishment. First-person testimony, in written form, by indentured immigrants is rare. Only three literary texts about the system of indenture that replaced slavery in the British empire, by laborers who experienced it personally, are known to exist. *Damra Phag Bahar*, or *Holi Songs of Demerara*, is the only one to emerge from the English-speaking Caribbean. The other two were memoirs by men from Fiji and Suriname.

It was in fact as a footnote that I first encountered Lalbihari Sharma. I learned about him while reading a scholarly monograph in June of 2011, during the final lap of research for my book *Coolie Woman*.[1] That book is partly a narrative history about indentured women in the Caribbean and partly a memoir about my attempts to uncover the mystery behind my own great-grandmother's exit from India in 1903 as a "coolie," or indentured laborer. She was born in the very same district in the very same region in the very same state in India as Sharma, and they came from the same caste background. The monograph's author, a Delhi-based labor historian, described the songbook as rich with sensory details about life on a sugar plantation in British Guiana from the perspective of an indentured man.

Here, finally, was the promise of indentured subjectivity that three years of intensive digging in archives had denied me. Here before me was the prospect of an indentured immigrant's inner life, in his own words. *Truly, passing reference was flesh.* It was enough to make my own flesh tingle. I could not have been any more thrilled, unless the anticipated words had been those of an indentured woman—or unless they had been in English. *Holi Songs* is written in the Devanagari script and in a combination of Awadhi and Bhojpuri, the idioms of the northern India regions that sent the most indentured immigrants abroad, as well as in Braj Bhasha, the literary language in which medieval poet-saints from India's Hindu heartland wrote.

Tracking down these words, in any language, proved no easy task. The labor historian in Delhi did not have an English translation of the text to share with me. The British Library, where I had researched much of my book, appeared to hold a single rare, original copy of the pamphlet in its repository of manuscripts belonging to the India Office, an administrative unit of the British empire. My first attempts to order the songbook using the shelfmark in the archive's catalog were thwarted. The item appeared to be lost. Crestfallen and in denial, I persisted nonetheless. Ultimately, an archivist, thinking creatively, succeeded in locating the songbook in a sheaf with other Hindi pamphlets at the library's off-site warehouse in far-off Yorkshire. She had bad news to temper the good, however: the paper was too acidic and brittle to be photo-copied. It was so delicate that it would not have survived the process. A month passed. I went home to the United States. And I kept coaxing from afar. In the end, the archivist scanned the pamphlet's 37 pages using special means and slipped them to me against protocol. I won't name her here, not even in footnotes—I don't want to land her in trouble for skirting the rules—but we are all in her debt. Without her, this translation would not exist.

Others have been instrumental, too. When I entrusted my copy of the songbook to my friend Rajiv Mohabir, with the request that he recreate it as a literary text in English, I also gave him a guide to work from: a translation cobbled together in a collaborative effort that began informally in the yard of an elderly man in a village in the Caroni plains of Trinidad. In August 2011, when the archivist sent me a digital copy of the original songbook, I was on the island listening to decades-old audio tapes of interviews with the last living indentured women there. A guide took me to Rohit Dass, the grandson of indentured immigrants from India who is also an itinerant reader of the *Ramayan*. In this capacity, he goes to homes where religious storytelling sessions are being held and reads from from the version of the ancient Hindu epic composed by the sixteenth-century poet-saint Tulsidas—the version most alive to the indentured, and the version that inspired much of Sharma's imagery and word choice in *Holi Songs*. Dass was the first to unlock the text for me. As I rocked in his hammock in the West Indies, where the songbook was composed, he translated out loud, and I scribbled notes.

Using these notes, I worked with a woman who, like the songbook's author, had been born in Bihar, ultimately producing the translation I used as a source for *Coolie Woman*. I then hired Shashwata Sinha, an immigrant to the United States who now teaches English composition in Ohio and who grew up in India listening to her maternal grandmother's folk tales and her mother's childhood stories. Sinha traces her maternal line to an

Awadhi-speaking area. She arrived at her understanding of Bhojpuri, the songbook's other primary language, as a bride. Her husband's family comes from Sharma's district in Bihar. Sinha was rigorous and hard-working, and brought to this project an ear tuned to spoken vernacular and the ways in which even the archaic language of the songbook still lives in the intimate interiors of memory and family.

Ashutosh Kumar, a young scholar of indenture, helped with a passage or two that Shashwata was unsure about, and I used my own knowledge of Guianese plantation terrain and vocabulary to make sense of details they could not untangle. They could not, for instance, be expected to know that Manja was Guianese Creolese for plantation manager and that Manja Darbar likely meant not a courtly assembly of dignitaries and entertainers but the weekly gathering of laborers at the manager's pay-table. Sometimes, in writing this translation together with Shashwata, I tried to elaborate in English what I felt must have been the emotion or worldview undergirding a word in Bhojpuri or Awadhi. For instance, I rendered the hat that a whip-bearing overseer wears as he rides into a field of workers as a "white man's tall hat / like a helmet / high on his head," because the specific word used conjured a pith helmet, headgear closely associated with colonialism and usually worn by white men doing empire's bidding in the fields. Such liberties are part of the alchemy of translation, especially when multiple people work together to decode a text.

The translation you have in your hands has its own separate alchemy, with Rajiv's prodigious gifts the catalytic agent. I felt strongly that these words should be out in the world in English, for the descendants of indenture and anyone else interested in their history. I asked Rajiv to translate the songbook's original rough translation because his skills and magic as a poet who gyaffs with— maybe even quarrels with—the muse of history made him the ideal custodian of this project. I also felt sure that, given his scholarly and artistic work with his own grand-mother's folk songs, as well as his reverence for orality, he would do it justice.

The *Ramcharitmanas*, the version of the many existing *Ramayans* that most guides Sharma's book, was kept alive on the plantations as well as in the villages of India for centuries prior to indenture by the devotees who would recite it. A community, speaking or singing this work, kept it alive, and no doubt also transformed it. A community, in a sense, was its author. And so, when Sharma takes a recurring line from the epic to describe the mental state of an indentured laborer when delivered from indenture, when he compares that mindset to the rapture of the mythical chakora bird feeding off moonbeams, he is presenting a metaphor composed in a sense collectively by generations and captured in the sixteenth century by Tulsidas. In the *Ramcharitmanas*, Tulsidas compulsively compared the love of the exiled prince Rama (an incarnation of Hinduism's preserver god Vishnu) for his wife Sita to the chakora's need for the moon. The chakora is the figurative lover, and the moon, the beloved. The lover's longing for the absent beloved serves as an allegory for man's pining for the unattainable divine, as in the Vaishnavite bhakti tradition of ballads about unfulfilled desire and the separation of lovers. Sharma appropriates this trope of the chakora and the moon to British Guiana's plantations and adds a new layer of meaning to it. In indenture's landscape, the absent beloved might, as Rajiv suggests, be India. Or it might be freedom. In either case, we now hand the chakora and the moon to another generation, one that speaks and reads English, just as generations before had handed the metaphor to Sharma for his own purposes. The collective nature of the endeavor is intact.

In *Coolie Woman*, I read the songbook as a source for the interior lives of indentured men: that is, to show the crises of faith that assailed them in their new setting. Sharma describes British Guiana as a "country of wrongdoing." The exterior landscape was overshadowed by the figure of the overseer with a whip in one hand and another, more subtle instrument of punishment in the other: the book in which he marked the names of laborers who failed to complete their allotted task and therefore risked both their day's pay and prison. The hovering prospect of being beaten, jailed, or docked wages drove the indentured to doubt. They felt deceived and misled by their gods. They felt like strays from their own religion. Sharma speaks of—seems, in fact, to confess to—immoral acts, shame, abandoned dharma and degraded karma. The interior landscape was a demoralized one.

Holi Songs was one tool I could use to humanize men who had committed monstrous acts, to place them in the context of battered masculinities and the anomie of plantation society. I interpreted the songbook, along with folk songs, oral histories, and the *Ramayan*, to try to make sense of the chilling crimes against indentured women by partners or would-be partners who used their cutlasses from the cane fields to mutilate and murder in retaliation for sexual agency exercised by the women. The nose, a symbol of honor, was often the target in attacks. My chapter about this spectacular violence, "Beautiful Woman Without a Nose," takes its title from a line in Sharma's songbook. As the indentured coped with the hardships and suffering of plantation life, Sharma urged them to take refuge in religion. "Without chanting the name of Rama," he preached, "the world is like a beautiful woman with her nose chopped off." The songbook allowed me to speculate that indenture might have imperiled the faith of migrants while making it more imperative than ever. The system threw them into the arms of their god at the same time as it made madmen of them. Sharma's songbook captures their cognitive dissonance.

A COMPLICATED FIGURE

In the final analysis, *Holi Songs of Demerara* is a conservative text.[2] It does not advocate overthrowing any hierarchies: of the plantation, of caste, of gender. Instead,

Sharma advises seeking solace in Rama and in the old order of village India, where the sardar was in charge. He warns that the rapture of freedom could go very wrong: so many roam without direction when released from indenture, like wandering beggars without a plan. Sharma instructs them instead to be patient "as before in the village" (to use Rajiv's translation) and to obey the sardar, so that their hearts might be content.

The songbook's fundamental defense of the status quo, even as it evokes sahibs with whips and prisons that unjustly jailed so many of the indentured, was a puzzle to me. The only other first-person account of indenture that circulated while the system was still in place was used as part of Gandhi's campaign to dismantle it. In fact, *My Twenty-One Years in the Fiji Islands* wasn't written by Totaram Sanadhya, the Gandhi disciple and ex-indentured laborer named as its author, but was told by him to another Gandhi disciple, a Bengali journalist who then crafted the autobiography. In this, it was akin to slave narratives, many of which were ghost-written testimonies deployed by abolitionists to attack slavery. *My Twenty-One Years*, like Sharma's songbook, offers the story of Rama's exile from his father's kingdom as an allegory for indenture. And the two accounts were published in India within a year of each other. *Holi Songs* was first printed in Bombay in 1915 by the Sri Venkateshwar Steam Press, one of the primary publishers of religious materials in India in the early twentieth century.[3] I wondered whether Sharma's book might have circulated in the same way as the Fiji account—and for the same reason—i.e. to arouse moral outrage against indenture as an affront to the honor of Indians. I also wondered how the songbook had made its way to India in the first place.

An invocation by Sharma led me into a labyrinth of research and speculation. As he prostrates himself before the gods at the songbook's start, he also pays obeisance to a Pandit Parmanand. Rajiv's translation describes the pandit, who also lived at Golden Fleece, as "renowned both here and abroad." There was indeed a Bhai Parman-and who lived in Guiana shortly before the songbook was published and who would soon become well known in revolutionary circles that stretched from the U.S. West Coast to the Indian subcontinent. Parmanand was a Punjabi missionary for the Arya Samaj, a reformist Hindu movement that challenged caste and child marriage and advocated for equality for women and the right of widows to remarry. In 1911, he lectured throughout Guiana. He had done the same in South Africa, where he got to know Gandhi, even living with him for a month. In Guiana, and in nearby Trinidad, Parmanand made the first inroads for the Arya Samaj movement. To counter the influence of Christian missionaries, he established the King George Hindu School in a house in the Guianese capital donated by a Brahmin who had become rich after indenture.

After a year laying this groundwork for the Arya Samaj, Parmanand left Guiana and made his way to San Francisco to study pharmacy. California, Oregon, and Washington were at the time hotbeds of activity by Punjabi immigrants, from lumber mill workers to elite students, agitating for India's independence through the underground revolutionary Ghadar Party. U.S. intelligence agents kept a surveilling eye on suspected members.

Parmanand was drawn into this network through a close friend who co-founded it. The revolutionaries plotted to provoke Indian soldiers in the British Army to mutiny during the First World War. Hundreds of immigrants from the U.S. returned to India to ignite this pan-Indian revolt. By 1914, Parmanand had returned home to the Punjab, where many of the conspirators turned to him to exchange currency and to communicate with each other. When the plot imploded in spectacular failure, Parmanand was one of nearly 300 men who were arrested and tried. In 1915, he was sentenced to life imprisonment on the Andaman Islands, off the southern coast of India.

In his revolutionary and reformist circuits, Parmanand had traveled by steamer across Europe, the Caribbean,

America, and then back to India. Had he perhaps taken the handwritten manuscript for *Damra Phag Bahar* on that journey with him? I can only follow a trail of coincidences and echoes to lay out the possibility. In his memoir, *The Story of My Life*, Parmanand briefly sketches his year in Guiana. He landed by steamer and was directed to a Hindu temple in an outpost of Indians free from indenture, about a mile outside the capital. He told the priest there that he was a Brahmin who had come from the motherland. The priest asked whether a new shipment of coolies had docked. He was puzzled to hear that Parmanand had not arrived indentured. This was an uncommon occurrence. Parmanand exchanged his hat and trousers for a turban and a dhoti, dress that more closely mirrored the Indians around him, and slept on the floor of the temple. An Indian he describes as "poor-looking" brought him rice and dal to eat. Parmanand took note of the man's intelligence; he was a reader of the *Venkateshwar* newspaper from Bombay. (This paper was a weekly published by the same press that later printed *Holi Songs of Demerara*. Could this unnamed Indian have been Lalbihari Sharma? I could not help but dream points of contact into the gaps.) At nightfall, after their day's work was done, Indian laborers would go to the temple to talk with Parmanand. He asked them whether there were any educated, well-known Hindus in the area, and they took him to a merchant born in Guiana. Through this man's connections, Parmanand arranged to speak at Town Hall in the capital. The newspapers ran notices announcing that a pandit from India would deliver a lecture. Thousands of Indians from distant villages flocked to hear him.

Parmanand identified the crucial merchant as Bihari Shaw and said the man visited him while he was imprisoned on the Andaman Islands. It seems likely, however, that he got the name wrong. There is no archival trace of a Bihari Shaw. But there was a prominent Hindu merchant in Georgetown, who, by 1904, owned a large retail business selling "East Indian and fancy goods" along the capital's main commercial thoroughfare. His name was Parbu Sawh. And he did visit India in 1919—the year before Parmanand was released early, in a show of clemency—as part of an official delegation exploring options for Indians to immigrate freely to the sugar colony after indenture ended.

The possible import of this became clear only recently, when I interviewed Sharma's grandson, a retired medical doctor living in Canada. He had reached out to me looking for a copy of the songbook. "We lost it a long time ago in Guiana," Sankar Sahai told me, ruefully. The last time he had seen the pamphlet was circa 1939, when he was a boy. He had used the book for the purpose it had been intended: as a kind of missal, a script from which to sing songs of longing and pleasure to celebrate the spring religious festival of Phagua, or Holi. In the riot of water and colored powder that mark the festival, the family's copy of the songbook got wet and was torn and ruined. In these conversations, Sahai revealed that his grandfather Lalbihari Sharma had been a "driver" on his sugar plantation, Golden Fleece. He was the figure referred to in the songbook as the sardar, a sort of Indian sub-overseer, an intermediary between the coolies and their white masters. I had known Sharma was Brahmin and therefore likely to have had the privilege of caste. But I had not known that he was part of the power structure of the plantation. He had left India as an indentured laborer, but he was a far more complicated and privileged a figure than I had once imagined.

I learned from his grandson that Sharma had bought three abandoned sugar estates along Guiana's Essequibo Coast in around 1910 and turned them into rice farms. He then leased out three-acre parcels to laborers he had known at Golden Fleece to farm as sharecroppers. He also tore down the derelict barracks where the indentured had lived communally on the plantation and erected respectable family houses on stilts. He loaned his tenant farmers the money required for mortgages on the houses he had built. He was thus their landlord and their money-lender and, as a pandit and a reader of the Tulsidas *Ramayan*, also their religious leader. In this system, many were financially indebted to Sharma and handed over all their earnings to him at the end of every harvest. His grandson who contacted me, born out of wedlock to Sharma's eldest son, grew up with his maternal grandparents in one of the tenant houses that Sharma had built. "They, too, were locked in this prison of poverty and indebtedness," Sahai shared.

In addition to everything else it revealed, this family history unlocked a tantalizing web of intermeshed relationships that suggest that Sharma might very well have crossed paths with Parmanand. The merchant who had helped the missionary begin his lecturing tour in Guiana, and who later visited him in India, was connected to Sharma by deep ties of marriage and plantation history. Sawh's daughter married Sharma's eldest son. And Sawh's father, the founder of the family business, had been indentured at Golden Fleece, the very plantation where Sharma had been a sardar. The Sawhs were rice millers as well as merchants, and the elder Sawh owned rice lands connected to Sharma's. Of course, I have no way of knowing whether or not the Pandit Parmanand described by Sharma in his songbook as the foundation of his being is the same man who circumnavigated the world of anti-colonial resistance. Neither can I say whether *Damra Phag Bahar* made its way to a religious printer in India in Parmanand's care. What I can say with confidence is that its author was a prominent man with firm ties to both the governing and the religious establishment.

At some point before the 1920s, as he became wealthier, Sharma changed his name from Lalbihari to Rashbihari. I don't know why he changed his name. It could have been that indenture authorities had mislabeled him. This often happened. I will parenthetically note, however, without drawing any conclusions, that Rashbihari Bose was a well-known Bengali freedom fighter who was involved in the failed Ghadar plot to incite Indian soldiers to mutiny and who was also wanted by the British for an attempt to assassinate the Indian viceroy in 1912. His fame might certainly have made it to Guiana to inspire a sympathizer with Indian self-determination.

Whatever the story behind this name-change might be, by the mid-1920s, official registers in Guiana listed the rechristened Rashbihari as one of the colony's principal rice and coconut growers and one of its biggest property owners of Indian origin. In 1925, the local governing board made him chairman of the district where his rice farm, named Johanna Cecilia, was based. In 1926, he founded the East Indian Burial Society, a co-op where people pooled money to pay for each other's funerals. The colony's major newspaper described him as "interested in the progress of his people." Bihari owned enough property to appear on the list of paid jurors in 1928. During Phagua celebrations that same year, *The New Daily Chronicle* noted that he gave a dinner for hundreds of Indians at his residence. And the following year, when Gandhi's acolyte, C.F. Andrews, visited the colony, a visit that resulted in his *Impressions of British Guiana*, Bihari threw a banquet in the anti-colonial crusader's honor. Five hundred Indians, wearing traditional attire, attended. Throughout the evening, they spoke to each other in Hindi. Some told Andrews that they were determined to visit India so as to learn about their mother country. Andrews wrote of the evening:

> There was such universal happiness as I have never seen before among East Indians of this colony. Everyone was deeply moved by the occasion.... Pundit Rash Behari is the leader of this district and he has become the chief religious authority along the Coast. It is very important, indeed, to get such leaders as he is wherever that is possible and to utilize them to the full. It has been a very great blow that since the time when I had written these notes, Pundit Rash Beharry has passed away.

This is the author of the songbook you hold in your hands. He is not the subaltern I expected. His grandson tells me that he was an orthodox Hindu, not a member of the Arya Samaj. In fact, the publisher who printed the songbook also published tracts attacking the reformist movement. The songbook may not have taken the route to India that I dreamily mapped in my head. He may simply have paid for the pamphlets to be printed in India and shipped back to Guiana. The songbook may not have circulated as part of the campaign against indenture. They may simply have been a missal for Phagua celebrations. Still, these words made the journey from orality to text, and they survive as testament to the complexity of a system and a man. Footnotes did know him well, however. That's how I found out about his property holdings and his status as a juror and district chairman: through footnotes in a decades-old dissertation. Whatever his privilege, all who are as descendants of indenture are footnoted when Sharma is footnoted. All of us are written into history. And when he is translated, all of us are translated.

<hr />

This essay originally appeared on the *Los Angeles Review of Books* website (www.LAReviewofBooks.org) as "Rescued From the Footnotes of History: Lal Bihari Sharma's *Holi Songs of Demerara* on March 20, 2018.

[1] Mohapatra, Prabhu P., "The Politics of Representation in the Indian Labour Diaspora: West Indies, 1880-1920," Delhi: V.V. Giri National Labour Institute, 2004.

[2] Mohapatra notes this conservatism in the songbook as well.

[3] Although the title page reads, "Published by the author, 11 February, 1916," the pamphlet's cover and the British Library's cataloguing of it both point to its first printing in 1915 by Khemraj Krishnadas, who ran the Sri Venkateshwar Steam Press, one of the oldest publishers of religious material in India.

Translating as a Practice
of Transformation
Translator's Note · *Rajiv Mohabir*

I began writing poetry when I was eight, building my own ideas of metaphor and image from the sun-dried bricks of folk music I knew. I do not come from a very literate household—in fact, my own paternal grandparents and my maternal great-grandparents were not able to read or write. My family came to Guyana to work the sugar plantations of Lusignan and Skeldon, bound by their own thumbprints on English contracts. But this did not mean that they did not possess a vast knowledge of their worlds.

I did not at first recognize my own writing as poetry; I thought of it as a record of my thoughts, written in a way that would be inaccessible to prying eyes. Poetry became a serious practice for me only after I started to learn my Aji's language, which is a form of Bhojpuri—a dialect of Hindi spoken in the states of Bihar and Uttar Pradesh in India. Through her language, she taught me songs. Her music dazzled me. I did what I could to learn it, recording her songs and speaking with her in Bhojpuri every chance I had, hopeful that this would help me learn a little more of what she knew.

I began the process of translating in my early twenties as an undergraduate focused on religious studies. That is when I realized that my Aji's language was a key to the culture of being Indo-Caribbean. The Bhojpuri that she had always spoken and sung was not standard Hindi but a new kind of language, one that had been created on sugar plantations and estates by indentured laborers and their children. My Aji was the last of our family who spoke Bhojpuri as a first language; due to its low social status, it had been abandoned in my parents' generation.

I think this made me love it even more. It was a language unique to our community, which had survived and persisted despite one hundred and thirty years of living in the diaspora, of being told that everything about our identities was broken, that we spoke "broken" English and "broken" Hindi. It was thus my own personal, live connection to South Asian culture. I clung to every word of it I could find.

But one thing troubled me as both a scholar and a translator. I studied in the West, where the written word is the measure by which cultures are evaluated. Yet most of the traditions I had experienced were oral. This absence of written texts meant that any attempt to render the language of my Aji visible would require a measure of creative invention.

So when Gaiutra Bahadur wrote me to ask if I would be interested in translating these verses, the only known literary record of indenture written in Awadhi/Braj Bhasha/Bhojpuri in the Anglophone Caribbean, I almost fell out of my chair. It seemed an answer to a question I had never even dared to ask myself. Here was a text written in the very language that I felt was not just ancestral but an actual ancestor. It even mentioned Demerara, one of the places my family is from in Guyana.

Gaiutra had written about these songs in her book *Coolie Woman: the Odyssey of Indenture*, and she had even undertaken a rough draft of an English-language translation, which she provided to me to look over. But more surprises were to be found once I was able to view the scanned copies of the original work for myself. When I opened to the first page, I that saw the folk songs were written not in standard Hindi, nor in the familiar lilt and rhythm of my Aji's Bhojpuri. Rather, the language of the text Gaiutra provided me mirrored the classical Braj Bhasha used by the great sixteenth-century Hindu devotional poets.[1] I began to understand that I held in my hands a new genre of devotional poem, one that was rooted in the Caribbean instead of India.

A NEW GENRE OF HINDU DEVOTIONAL POETRY

To fully appreciate the remarkableness of this work, it is important to understand the context in which it was written.

Hindu devotional poetry draws upon a tradition that is perhaps most closely associated with medieval India, when writers such as Kabir, Surdas, and Mirabai, known as bhakti poets, revolutionized the formulaic, ritualistic practice of the Hindu religion as enacted by upper-caste (Brahmin) pandits and pujaris (priests). By sixteenth century, when Kabir, one of the most famous bhakti poets, is purported to have lived and worked as a weaver, Hindus were at a crossroads of sorts, their temples being demolished by monotheists in the North. At issue was increasing dissatisfaction with the caste system.[2] The Brahmin or priestly class—the only ones authorized to perform the rituals and sacrifices required for the appeasement of the Vedic gods—often demanded significant fees to perform the ceremonies and prayers necessary to a proper ordering of the world. Without the Brahmins, these ceremonies and prayers would remain incomplete. However, this system also served to keep the castes separated. Many non-Brahmins chose to convert to the newly introduced religion of Islam, which taught that it was possible to speak to god without an intermediary. Others, many of them poets, pioneered a new way of relating to god within the Hindu context, addressing god as the Self, or in the case of the legendary bhakti poet Mirabai, as a lover.

These bhakti poets, or devotional poets, opened up a new world of possibility, one in which there was no more need for pandits, Brahmins, and temple charlatans. Instead, one could speak directly to god through song and prayer. In the poetry of this movement, all caste or religious distinctions, or indeed any other label that might separate one person from another, are considered to be a result of maya, that great illusion that keeps us thinking that we are not already with god, that we live lives separate and distinct from one another.

Because I'd spent time translating bhakti poetry in Jaipur and Varanasi, I quickly realized that Sharma's work had been composed by someone educated in medieval Indian poetry. This came as something as a shock to me. In all my studies and in all my familial stories, I had never been made aware that indentured laborers might have had this kind of sophisticated education. For me, this is important because it goes against certain popular mis-conceptions. Most people believe that those who ended up indentured in the Caribbean were uneducated, duped by the British into working their colonial fields. But while many of those who chose to migrate were in fact illiterate, the indisputable, published fact of Sharma's songs shows that the situation was far more complicated.

These inheritances—this complexity—have however been largely lost. Not only are most Indo-Caribbean poetics derived from languages and cultures that are neither Bhojpuri nor Awadhi, but the colonial rupture of indentured servitude, and the alienation from languages that it led to, has meant that the people of the Caribbean have had to rebuild their cultures in English, the language of social prestige. As a result, the poetry taught in schools has been that of daffodils or other flora and fauna alien to a Caribbean landscape. Meanwhile, the meanings of folksongs and the particular customs that they belong to have been viewed as a kind of occult knowledge, one not supported by mainstream religion or cultural values.

Yet Sharma's songs give us an alternate view into the world of diasporic experience. The religiosity and sophistication I saw in his writings not only amazed me, it changed the landscape of my poetic imaginary. Born in England and raised in the United States, I had been told all my life that we come from a "broken" tradition. This text showed me a mirror—it showed me my face in one solid piece.

POETIC FORMS USED BY LALBIHARI SHARMA

The poetic forms that Lalbihari Sharma includes in *I Even Regret Night: Holi Songs of Demerara*—chaupai, chautal, doha, kavitt, ulara, and bhajan—are derived from folksong, and each possesses its own structures and history rooted in performance and narrative tradition. They are celebratory in nature, and capacious enough to contain epic narratives as well as songs of praise. Typically sung during Phagua/Holi, they are performed by two lines of singers that face one another and sing back and forth different varieties of Phagua songs (songs of the holiday), each with its own particular pattern of vigor and rest.

In order to make accessible to the reader some of these forms that I have migrated into English through this translation, I present herewith a brief guide.

Bhajan: This is a type of devotional song that does not have a set metrical structure. Bhajans often contain lyrics that praise deities and can be used as part of religious worship ceremonies. Since they are written in the vernacular and not in Sanskrit, they are intended for use by lay people. Included in Sharma's text are two types of devotional bhajans. One is dedicated to the physical representation of god who comes to earth in bodily form. This style of bhajan is known as sagun bhakti, or devotion to the god that has form. The second is the bhajan in praise of the unseen god that pervades all things—the deity that is formless and inside us all. This is known as nirgun bhakti. Bhajans typically vary widely in rhythm and style, and can be sung to various ragas and tunes.

Chhand: A poem written as a quatrain. These are usually declarative in nature and used ceremoniously in praise of a specific person. In this collection, the chhand are used to introduce the poet Lalbihari Sharma, identifying his place of origin and telling us a little about where he is from as a way of establishing his credibility.

Chaupai: Literally a quatrain written in two lines with a meter of four main beats per section and sixteen syllables per line. This is the most common form used for narrative poetry. Sharma's use of the chaupai structure pays homage to the great bhakti poet Tulsidas, who composed his famous *Sri Ramcharitmanasa*, a rendition of the *Ramayan* in the vernacular Awadhi, using this form. Other classical examples of the chaupai include the "Hanuman Chalisa," a prayer to the monkey god.

Chautal: Literally four claps in the structure. This type of meter, which describes an entire subset of songs, is comprised of fourteen beats and is used when performing songs around Holi. Chautal songs are practiced in the Caribbean and also in villages in the Bhojpuri belt in India, namely Bihar and Uttar Pradesh.[3] This style of singing is well-documented by the late Indo-Caribbean drummer and musician Rudy Ramnarine and the ethnomusicologist Peter Manuel in their collection of chautal songs, *Chowtal Rang Bahar: A Treasury of Chowtal Songs From India and the Caribbean.* However, according to scholars, the practice of chautal has been diminishing in recent times, drowned out by the catchier and ubiquitous music of Bollywood.[4]

Doha: A rhyming couplet written with a 11/13 beat and 11/13 syllabation. A notable doha writer is Kabir, whose bhakti poetic tradition is threaded throughout Sharma's work.

Kavitt: A poem written in quatrains whose rhythm is meant to correspond with the movements of a kathak dancer. In the songs presented here, Sharma deviates from the strict quatrain form of the kavitt, using its syllabation patterns but without ensuring the completeness of the four lines.

Ulara:	A short three to four line song that follows a chautal, but is usually lighter in tone and semantic significations. This indicates the chorus-like patter of gol singing that takes place during Holi. The ularas in this collection are highly repetitive and indicate the quality of repetitive recitation that offers a lyric respite from the more complicated and demanding performance of chautal.

A TRANSLATOR'S CHOICES

As a translator, I deal with a palimpsest of silences. While some translators feel compelled to "foreignize" their English, as Walter Benjamin insists, others strive to preserve the integrity of a line's music, allowing all kinds of gaps in meaning. The South Asian forms that Sharma writes in depends upon the stresses of the Awadhi and Bhojpuri languages, a reservoir of cadence not available in the English language. Implicit cultural and political presumptions further vex translations that are mediated by colonial relationships—in this case, the power play that inevitably exists between colonial-era Hindustani poetry and the English language. In his book *Flesh and Fish Blood: Postcolonialism, Translation, and the Vernacular*, postcolonial scholar and translator Subramanian Shankar insists that translation must be read as a practice of "interpretation rather than rendering." Gayatri Chakravorti Spivak, in her article, "The Politics of Translation," says that translation—especially when pertaining to songs in Indic languages—is an act that must be undertaken in a way that considers the author: the newly migrated text must be comprehensible to the writer of the original, keeping the same register of language and tone.

The works presented here were originally meant as songs, as a living part of an oral culture. So by attempting this translation, I had been tasked with transforming a text meant for music into one that belongs to an entirely different world. Part of the translation process has thus been carving these poems, originally intended to be worn in throats and ears, into forms that they could inhabit on a printed page.

I have attempted to address these issues by taking a cue from Borges, who says, "the original is unfaithful to the translation." Instead of relying on the metrical structures of the South Asian language presented by Sharma, I have attempted to translate meanings more closely to the semantic significations of the text. And in order to make these songs, originally published without any line breaks, read more like poems, I have changed their lineation to reflect their musicality. This has allowed me as translator more room in the text, making possible more twists of meaning.

I have thus chosen to format each style of poem in ways that I hope help to honor and pay homage to the type of song it references. My intention in so doing has been to transform these poems and make available their original meaning without having to adhere so fixedly to the structure of the form. For example, the dohas are translated as couplets and the chaupals are written into quatrains. This is something I learned to do from reading Agha Shahid Ali's translations of the legendary Urdu poet Faiz Ahmad Faiz in *The Rebel's Silhouette*. Instead of preserving couplets as they appear in Faiz's Urdu, Ali broke Faiz's lines into pieces that fit his own sense of what the lines wanted to accomplish. This particular way of translating the musical tradition of South Asian poetry provided me the inspiration to translate Sharma's songs with a sense that is both intuitive and reflective of my own poetic practice.

Finally, to allay any fear of over-fidelity to the original language to the detriment of its musical origins, I have allowed myself to consider my translations as one of many possible avatars or emanations of the original text.

ON THE DAMRA JOURNEY THROUGH SPIRITUALITY
What is instantly remarkable about this collection is how, by embedding Indian poetic inheritances within

the realities of indentured diasporic experiences, Sharma manages a potent alchemy of philosophical guidance, musicality, and devotion.

As Bahadur's research tells us, Sharma was a sirdar, one of the drivers who kept other indentured laborers in line on the plantations. He thus saw firsthand, and perhaps even had a hand in, the trials and joys that his country folk suffered under the economic exploitation of the British in the period between 1838–1917. Indeed, this collection of songs begins by recalling the plantation experiences of those bonded by contract to work the earth and at the mercy of British planters.

At the same time, the use of the vernacular shows Sharma's work to be in conversation with bhakti devotional poets. Sharma is thus in effect reflecting upon the human condition according to Vedantic Hindu philosophy. Beyond creating a set of devotional songs tailored to the circumstances of Indo-Caribbean life, he is elaborating upon the soul's journey from the illusory (maya) to the Real.

If Sharma's songs start off with a consideration of the material conditions of plantation life and experiences, they soon attempt to escape those conditions through the the narration of sacred myth.

By relating stories in which the incarnated gods Krishna, Radha, Rama, and Sita play Holi and pine for one another, experiencing human emotions, Sharma is able to delve deep into the psychic realms of indentureship.

For example, in one of his "Chautal" poems, Sharma writes in the voice of Radha, Krishna's consort, as she waits at home for her lover to return:

From abroad Piya sends
no word. I'm listless in the month
of Phagun without my love.
The papiha bird cries out, piya—

I'm overcome by this distance between us.

He stole away to another country
without telling me. The rain falls
like arrows or serpents, stirring worry

in my heart.

By reinterpretating the Krishna myth in order to em-
ulate the pain of separation from one's beloved, Sharma
reflects the influence of the sixteenth century poet Mira-
bai, perhaps the most famous of the sagun bhakti poets.
In Mirabai's poems, the human soul is represented as a
woman whose beloved, the divine, is absent, the two sepa-
rated through illusion. According to the practice of sagun
bhakti, the only clear path to liberation and a merging
with the divine is through devotion to a specific form of
god, a god with form.

But in Sharma's poem, an implicit parallel is also
being made between exile and indenture, the separation
between the speaker and the beloved deepened and made
more complex by the circumstances of migration. The
speaker's description of longing could refer as much to
the distance between the indentured from their "home" as
to that between the human and the divine.

Sharma ends his collection with a series of bhajans that
show a spirituality that has shifted from embodying the
perspectives of the women in mythology to a more devo-
tional tone, taking the reader or listener into a personal
space where the deity is not one of flesh and bone, but
rather is simultaneously all-pervasive and seemingly ab-
sent. This turn to nirgun bhakti, or that form of devotion
that praises a god without form, connects Sharma's work
to the poetry and hymns written by or attributed to the
great bhakti poet-saint Kabir (1440-1518), whose religious
philosophy laments the duality of the Real and maya.
Kabir asserts that in order to escape the torture of illusion,
and to escape the bondage of karma that ties the soul into
the cycles of human incarnation and death, one must
chant the name of Rama.[5]

In his "Fourth Bhajan," the poet Sharma makes clear the connections between his spirituality and his poetic lineage:

Lalbihari is of no use;
you are alone and destitute.

This whole creation is a dreamlike
illusion. Sing the only truth

of Rama's name.

The name of the divine is Rama, but not in the sense of Rama the sagun deity, son of King Dasharatha and incarnation of Vishnu. Rather, Rama is invoked as a way of acknowledging the eternal life force, the god behind the gods, the master divinity that is beyond human understanding—the Real behind the maya. In these final poems, the soul is thus figured as eternal, escaping torment through devotion and by keeping righteous company. Sharma asks:

Without singing praises to Hari,
who will attain bliss?

In this move from the physical to the spiritual, Sharma the poet, the singer of songs, reconciles with the divine and shows his readers a clear path to liberation from suffering, offering help and advice along the way,

Sing these thoughts of Rama,
give up your attachments
and desires.

Lalbihari says, "Try and understand,
the company of saints is absolute truth."

POSITIONALITY AND POETRY

As a poet myself who is obsessed with the music of the Indian diaspora and specifically the music of my own tradition, working on this text has been revelatory. I have always charted my own poetic lineage from the chutney music of Sundar Popo and Dropati, music that itself took inspiration from the devotional populism of bhakti poetry. But in Sharma's combination of precision, spirituality, and clarity, I have been able to find the seed of a story that shows me how I myself can be transformed.

By describing the journey from the material into the spiritual, this collection as a whole functions as a kind of a guide, showing me possible ways of re-conceptualizing and re-framing a cultural inheritance and knowledge that colonial and postcolonial pressures to assimilate have caused to be devalued and eschewed, even by my own family of origin.

Given that South Asian languages rarely appear the world of postcolonial Caribbean literature, it is my sincerest hope that people come to this text understanding what this tradition of oral language gives to the Caribbean landscape. Our particular mix of South Asian languages has been almost entirely extinguished by the cultural hegemony of English. But by digging into Sharma's archive of sound, spirituality, and image, I have been able to see exactly how themes of separation have unfolded through to my own generation. My family has always been haunted by the unfulfilled contract that promised to return us to a homeland that no longer exists. What Sharma shows is that such a return is psychic, the return of the spirit to the "home," a merging with divinity in a way, that, though rooted in bondage, can be released to the sky. I grapple regularly with large questions such as these in my own poems: Where does the soul begin and where is it going? What is poetry if not a steady searching?

By reading and translating Sharma, I've learned to constantly engage with the materiality of sound as I attempt to reclaim what is lost to my generation. I have come to truly appreciate that in order to do so I must write in and out of all my languages: Guyanese Creole, English, and Bhojpuri. In Sharma's plantation Hindi, I hear echoes of my own ancestors singing for the spring of the soul, praying colors into play.

<hr />

[1] The languages that scholars agree have created modern Hindi include Braj Bhasha, Bhojpuri, and Awadhi—all non-standardized languages of North India, and all closely identified with the tradition of devotional poetry and music. Though seen to be more rustic and rooted in village life, these languages are, ironically, admired for their poetic depth and traditions.

[2] India has four major castes that are organized into a hierarchical structure that include Brahmins (the priestly class) at the top, then Kshatriyas (the ruling class), Vaishyas (the mercantile class), and Shudras (the servant class). Dalits fall outside of the caste system entirely, and suffer oppression from this system as a result.

[3] The chautal in particular is specific to Indo-Caribbean people—so much so that it became the forerunner to a new kind of Caribbean music with Indian roots: chutney music. During the 1960s, singers such as Sundar Popo and Yusef Islam sang bhakti poetry set to song and rhythm. In so doing, they brought the performance of folk music traditions to the public sphere, harkening back to the metaphors and experiences that had inspired their ancestors, but fitting them into the sonic landscape of the Caribbean. Following in the tradition of bhakti poets, these musicians found inspiration in the idea of liberation from caste and religion, but in the service of a new Caribbean cultural rebuilding.

[4] This could be due to Bhojpuri cinema's wild take off from obscurity to its present style of racy songs and dancing.

[5] Though Rama is the seventh incarnation of Vishnu, he is held to be the formless god.

WORKS CITED

Shankar, S. Flesh and Fish Bone: Postcolonialism, Translation, and the Vernacular. Berkeley: University of California Press. 2012.

Spivak, Gayatri Chakravorty. "The Politics of Translation." The Translation Studies Reader. New York: Routledge, 2000. 397-416.

Lalbihari Sharma was born in Chapra village in the United Provinces of India (now Bihar, India) and indentured by the British East India Company to work the sugarcane fields. A musician and singer, he published his chautal folksongs in 1916.

Gaiutra Bahadur's *Coolie Woman*, a personal history of indenture, was shortlisted for Britain's Orwell Prize, the international literary award for artful political writing. Her short fiction "The Stained Veil" appears in the 2018 Feminist Press anthology *Go Home!* Named a Nieman Fellow by Harvard for her work as a journalist, she has also been awarded literary residences at the MacDowell Colony and the Bellagio Center in Italy. She writes for *The New York Times Book Review*, *The New York Review of Books*, *VQR*, and *Dissent*, among other publications.

Rajiv Mohabir is the author of *The Cowherd's Son* (Tupelo Press 2017, winner of the 2015 Kundiman Prize) and *The Taxidermist's Cut* (Four Way Books 2016, winner of the Four Way Books Intro to Poetry Prize and finalist for the Lambda Literary Award for Gay Poetry in 2017). In 2015, PEN awarded him the PEN/Heim Translation Fund Grant Award for the completion of *I Even Regret Night: Holi Songs of Demerara*.

Photo Credits

The photographs published here are by Bror E. Dahlgren and have been reprinted courtesy of The Field Museum.

Page 20
At mouth of a drainage canal. CSB43768
© The Field Museum

Page 21
Young girl. CSB43543
© The Field Museum

Page 26
East India washer woman. CSB43791
© The Field Museum

Pages 27 and 208
Street with people. Palm trees. CSB43537
© The Field Museum

Pages 32 and 176
Returning from George-town market. CSB43738
© The Field Museum

Pages 33 and 136
East Indians at their breakfast. CSB43795
© The Field Museum

Pages 52 and 190
Road house construction, Gantry in background. CSB43755
© The Field Museum

Page 53
Man holding a termite nest. CSB43479
© The Field Museum

Page 137
Two young children, one crying. CSB43544
© The Field Museum

Acknowledgements

A world of thanks to Neelanjana Banerjee, Sunyoung Lee, and all of the folks at Kaya Press who saw the value in the re-singing of these songs in a North American context. A special thank you to Ziyi Xu for designing this book with such patience and care.

Thank you to Gaiutra Bahadur who asked me if I would be able to translate this volume.

Thank you to Amar Ramessar who has put some of these songs to music.

Thank you to the PEN/Heim Translation Fund Grant Award without whose help this would not have been possible.

Several of these translations have appeared in *Modern Poetry in Translation*, *Jacket2*, *Asymptote Journal* and *PEN America*.